Of all poetic forms, the limerick
steadfastly remained thoroughly
clean-up attempts. Ballads once
lyrical, romantic and frequently insipid, folk doggerel is
often tainted with over-earnest social criticism; no poetic
form has emerged through the centuries with the 'purity' of
the limerick. And because it is the only kind of verse which
permits blatant filth, lewdness is all the more concentrated.
In this encyclopaedic collection presented by Panther Books
in two volumes, every imaginable smutty topic is covered,
from Buggery to Zoophily, from Abuses of the Clergy to
Oral Irregularity. *The Limerick* supersedes all other
collections and is a must for anyone who appreciates this
fine and demanding art.

In addition, Volume I contains a detailed, fascinating survey
of the development of the limerick and its triumph over
those who have tried to bowdlerize it, from its earliest
appearance in the fourteenth century to present-day
examples.

G. Legman
Editor

The Limerick

Volume I

Panther

Granada Publishing Limited
Published in 1976 in two volumes by Panther Books Ltd
Frogmore, St Albans, Herts AL2 2NF

First published in Great Britain in one volume by
Jupiter Books (London) Ltd 1974
Copyright © 1964, 1969 by G. Legman
Made and printed in Great Britain by
Richard Clay (The Chaucer Press) Ltd, Bungay, Suffolk
Set in Monotype Times

CONTENTS

INTRODUCTION
TO THE LIMERICK

Known to everyone, but its paternity admitted by very few, the bawdy limerick has held its place now, for exactly a century, as the chosen vehicle of cultivated, if unrepressed, sexual humor in the English language. As almost nothing that has been written about the limerick can be taken seriously – which is perhaps only fitting – a few words may not be out of place here, as to its real history, its origins, and its century of triumph, by way of celebrating the centenary of that triumph.

The limerick is, and was originally, an indecent verse-form. The 'clean' sort of limerick is an obvious palliation, its content insipid, its rhyming artificially ingenious, its whole pervaded with a frustrated nonsense that vents itself typically in explosive and aggressive violence. There are, certainly, aggressive bawdy limericks too, but they are not in the majority. Except as the maidenly delight and silly delectation of a few elderly gentlemen, such as the late Langford Reed, and several still living who might as well remain nameless, the clean limerick has never been of the slightest real interest to anyone, since the end of its brief fad in the 1860s. Nor has this fad ever been successfully revived by the periodic advertising contests, exciting amateur versifiers to hack together clean limericks by the tens of thousands. It should be observed in this connection, and despite the continuous devaluation of any monetary sum over the sixty years past, that were a prize to be offered here of £3 a week *for life*, as has been given for a limerick last line, in a British cigarette contest in 1907, the present writer could seriously demand and safely expect that thousands of unpoetic amateurs in Great Britain and the United States would slap themselves silly for the next six months or two years, trying to compose seven-line stanzas in spondaic hexameter – alternating with amphibrachs and amphimacers, if I felt like being cruel –

all seven lines to rhyme solely with the words *silver*, *swollen*, *spoilt*, and *sylph* (none of which have rhymes). Needless to say, the winning entry and all seventeen thousand losing entries would immediately and forever be forgotten, except by their authors, the moment the winner would be announced. Viable folk-poetry, and folk-poetic forms, cannot be created by any such cash-on-the-barrelhead methods.

The original limerick fad was accidentally created by the reprinting in London, in 1863, of Edward Lear's *Book of Nonsense*, a volume of very tepidly humorous limericks, illustrated by the author, that had first appeared nearly twenty years before, in 1846, without any extraordinary success. Inspired by the reprint however, *Punch*, the humorous English magazine, seized upon the form. The same was done in America by a minor writer and sedulous-ape, Charles Godfrey Leland, who later also embarrassingly imitated Lewis Carroll's *Alice in Wonderland* – illustrations, typography and all – in *Johnnykin and the Goblins* (1877). Leland's anonymous imitation of Lear was called *Ye Book of Copperheads*, and was published by Leypoldt in Philadelphia in 1863. It is entirely satirical, all its limericks being directed against the Northern 'copperhead' defeatists, and the anti-Lincoln agitations during the Civil War. In the same year there had also appeared a set of 'Nursery Rhymes for the Army', in Wilkes' *Spirit of the Times*, in New York; twenty-three limericks signed L.L.D., initials that may possibly represent Leland's name with the vowels omitted. A British imitation of Lear, which had perhaps sparked Leland's, was *Ye Book of Sense* (Torquay and London, 1863).

Almost immediately after, a much more widely circulated imitation appeared, this time acknowledging Lear's inspiration in the title, *The New Book of Nonsense*, being issued in Philadelphia in 1864 to be sold for the profit of the Sanitary Commission, the Red Cross of the Civil War. With that, the limerick fad was launched in America, though always under the name of 'nonsense rhymes' or 'nursery rhymes' until the 1880s, when, for the first time, the name *limerick* seems to have been applied to the form. The name is of unknown origin, having been appropriated from that of the town in Ireland for reasons never really explained, possibly from a now-forgotten chorus, 'Won't you come up to Limerick?'

The limerick metre was, in fact, very commonly used in songs in the Irish language, usually dedicated to liquor, love, or patriotism throughout the eighteenth century, as any collection of these will show. See, for numerous examples, Kathleen Hoagland's *1000 Years of Irish Poetry*. The form also appears in English in the Irish songs of Thomas Moore in the early nineteenth century, such as 'The Time I've Lost in Wooing', 'A Lottery', and 'The Young May Moon' (Quiller-Couch's *Oxford Book of English Verse*, No. 582), this last clearly inspired by Herrick's exquisite 'The Night-piece: To Julia', two centuries before, as will be seen. The Irish limericks are, in any case, very late in the history of the metrical form.

Other imitations came thick and fast after the American Sanitary Commission volume of 1864: *Ye Book of Bubbles* (which took even the 'Ye' of its title from Leland), *Inklings for Thinklings*, and at least one other proposed *Nonsense Book* to be illustrated by the children's artist, Susan Hale. The fatuousness into which the form immediately fell, without the excitements of the Civil War to get its teeth into, is pathetically betrayed in a letter from Miss Hale, as to her final volume of the sort, remarking: 'Mrs. Billy Weld ... provides, collects and invents the rhymes, and I draw the pictures right off into a nice long-shaped blank book. I have got 22 done, and they go off very fast, much quicker than the Nursery Rhymes for the fair, for the rhymes are only fool stuff ...'

Punch was similarly running 'fool stuff' in the 1860s, and might have gone on forever except that the fad of the clean limerick was suddenly brought to an end – owing to a disconcerting number of bawdy and sacrilegious limericks being submitted anonymously, among the entries to *Punch*'s first big geographical-limerick contest. According to a tradition, the leaders of this anti-fad, and authors of all the best early dirty limericks, which immediately began to circulate orally, of course, were a group of college wits and clubmen, notably the poet Swinburne; an army officer, Capt. Edward Sellon, and the war-correspondent, George Augustus Sala, all three of whom are known to have written much other sub-rosa poetry and erotic prose, mostly flagellational. *Punch* closed down its geographical contest with a slam, and the clean-limerick fad fell dead. It had lasted hardly five years, a great deal longer than most fads. Since that time, the clean limerick has lived on fitfully only as the last resource of newspaper poets (especially about the 1900s) hard-up for witty fillers, as a useful framework for humorous artists to hang their drawings on, and, as aforesaid, as advertising-contest pap from time to time. As for the public at large – that is to say, the authentic folklore transmitting group – the only real popularity of the limerick during the entire century of its modern existence, since the end of the Civil War, has been wholly and solely in the bawdy form.

A few assessments other than my own might perhaps not be out of place here. Langford Reed, who led with his chin in writing to all the literary panjandrums of the 1920s asking what they thought of his project of publishing a thoroughly expurgated *Complete Limerick Book* (London, 1924), was almost crushed under a chorus of plain statements like these: From Arnold Bennett: 'In reply to your letter, all I have to say about Limericks is that the best ones are entirely unprintable.' (The one about the Young Plumber of Leigh, No. 60 in Vol. II, was also nominated by Bennett as 'The best limerick of all.') From George Bernard Shaw: 'There are several personal limericks by D. G. Rossetti, and some by Swinburne, which became known in their generation, but like the large number of geographical limericks which preceded them they are mostly unfit for publication. They must be left for oral tradition . . .' Arthur Wimperis used fewer words to say a great deal more: 'The only limericks in my experience of any literary merit are distinctly Rabelaisian. Beside these, the more polite and printable examples fade away into the dim haze of mediocrity.'

On the other side of the Atlantic, the consensus of opinion has been the same. Don Marquis is reported to have divided limericks into three kinds (sometimes in rising order of price): 'Limericks to be told when ladies are present; limericks to be told when ladies are absent but clergymen are present – and LIMERICKS.' Prof. Morris Bishop, the unquestionable modern master in the clean limerick line, has put the essence of his art into verse, as half – and not really the better half – of his 'The Sonnet and the Limerick':

> The limerick is furtive and mean;
> You must keep her in close quarantine,
>   Or she sneaks to the slums
>   And promptly becomes
> Disorderly, drunk and obscene.

Finally, in William S. Baring-Gould's *The Lure of the Limerick* (New York: Clarkson N. Potter, Inc., 1967; London: Rupert Hart-Davis, 1968; Panther Books, 1971), the first publicly issued collection to combine both clean and bawdy examples, a mildly scatological limerick on tea-and-pee sent in to the Salada Tea contest in recent years is cited, p. 186 – it did not win! – with the observation: 'Mike Nichols, once asked to judge a limerick contest, is reported to have said: "It was easy. We just threw out the dirty limericks and gave the prize to the one that was left".'

Before continuing with the further history of the limerick which looks as though it will continue for quite a while yet, what about its pre-history? It has been tiresomely repeated, and is even partly true, that Lear took the form of his 'nonsense rhymes' from several illustrated children's books of the early 1820s: *Anecdotes and Adventures of Fifteen Gentlemen*, attributed to one R. S. Sharpe, and *The History of Sixteen Wonderful Old Women* of a competing publisher. (There was also a *Fifteen Young Ladies* collection too.) Actually, these 1820s limericks are far better than Lear's, and the drawings – probably by Robert Cruikshank – incomparably better. The specific rhyme known to have inspired Lear is the following, reproduced with its amusing illustration in Iona and Peter Opie's *Oxford Dictionary of Nursery Rhymes*, at 'Tobago'.

> There was a sick man of Tobago
> Liv'd long on rice-gruel and sago;
>   But at last, to his bliss,
>   The physician said this –
> 'To a roast leg of mutton you may go.'

The illustration shows him attacking the leg of mutton, which looks more like a ham, with a carving-fork and knife and a blissful expression. This poor chap evidently had gout, in the bad old days before Allo-purinol came to cut its suffering and its cruelly restricted diet.

Two other limericks from Sharpe's *Fifteen Gentlemen*, with their spirited illustrations, are reproduced in Philip James' and C. G. Holme's *Children's Books of Yesterday* (London: The Studio, 1933). These colored books of the 1820s, which appeared when Lear was eight or ten years old, and whose jolly illustrations are so much better than the overrated whimsy of his own feeble scratchings, are generally in the pure limerick form of the example cited above. Occasionally, as in one on a young man of St. Kitts, the last line repeats and commiserates with the hero of the opening line: 'Alas! poor young man of St. Kitts.' This repeated or unrhyming line is actually one of the oldest forms of the limerick stanza, and was already several centuries out of date by the 1820s.

Lear's imitation of this form, as is well known, invariably drops back, from the simple but dramatic resolution of the action in the final line, to the namby-pamby repetition of the first line – very weak, even for nonsense verse – made to do double duty as the last line as well, possibly with some tremendously unimportant change in the adjective rung in by way of climax. Lear also curiously betrayed, in many of his limericks, an insurmountable private fear of public disgrace (the only passions of his life being, unfortunately, for cats and handsome Greek boys), in the continuous importation into his couplets of the Mrs. Grundy of public opinion, in the horrendous and ever-present *They*: 'When they said, "Why is that?" He fell in his hat, That frightened old man of Corfu,' and so on. The whole thing, and most particularly the invariable echoic last line, represents a clear failure of nerve, an inability to take the obvious and final jump, and to resolve even the stated nursery situation in some satisfactory way. This is the neurotic problem at the root of all 'nonsense', and is – as much with Lewis Carroll as with Lear – the secret or Sense of Nonsense.

II

The pre-history of the limerick is remarkably easy to trace. It is necessary only to recognize, as modern developments not really essential to the limerick pattern, the anapestic form or foot (two short syllables and a long) in which it has become familiar, as well as the falsely stressed 'There *was* . . .' in the opening line, which is two centuries older than Lear in any case. The earliest limericks will be found in nursery rhymes, or something very much like them, as far back as the fourteenth century. To avoid controversy, I do not insist that 'Sumer is i-cumen in' (about 1300), the oldest popular song in the English language, is in the limerick form, but a rather good case can be made for its stanzaic portion at least, and the possibility ought not to be overlooked. In modernized spelling:

> Ewè bleateth after lamb,
> Low'th after calvè coo;
> Bullock starteth,
> Buckè farteth –
> Merry sing cuck*oo*!

With all that has been written about 'Sumer is i-cumen in' – and it has taken almost a library of learned annotation to vindicate even the simple barnyard humor of the buck's crepitation at the highest note and melodic climax of the song – no suggestion has ever yet been made as to just what its prosodic form may be; and where, and when, and whether any verses similar to it may be found, in any language.

In their excellent manual of the poet's craft, *The Making of Verse* (1934), p. 102, Robert Swann and Frank Sidgwick have discovered another early animal limerick (and that it is a limerick they clearly state) in the British Museum's Harleian Manuscript 7322, dating from the fourteenth century:

> The lion is wondirliche strong,
> & ful of wiles of wo;
> & wether he pleye
> other take his preye
> he can not do bot slo (*slay*).

This is followed in the manuscript by similar warning rhymes, as to dragons and bears, but not in the limerick metre. A century and a half then passes without record of this engaging form except perhaps in the 'Poulter's measure' or 'short metre' of Elizabethan hymnology, to be discussed below. The limerick form itself, still partly in iambic metre, reappears suddenly in the late sixteenth century, in the mad-songs of the half-naked wandering beggars, turned out to mump their livelihood after 1536, at the dissolution of the religious almonries under Henry VIII. Where it had lain in the meanwhile, and whether the madmen learned it from the musician-monks, or the monks from the madmen, there is now no way of knowing.

The mad 'Bedlams', as they were called, were still wandering and singing two hundred years later, in both England and Ireland, as recorded by the Irish poet and physician, Oliver Goldsmith (who is also believed to have been the first editor of the *Mother*

Goose rhymes in English), in his play *The Good Natur'd Man* in
1768, III.ii.4–9, where Honeywood asks his servant for his brown
and silver suit of clothes, only to be told: 'That, your honour gave
away to the begging gentleman that makes verses, because it was
as good as new.' The greatest of the mumpers' songs is 'Mad
Tom', or 'Tom o' Bedlam', first recorded in Giles Earle's manuscript music-book about 1615, though probably decades old by
then, and in the limerick metre throughout, to a tune as haunting
as the words:

> From the hagg & hungry Goblin,
> That into raggs would rend yee,
>   & the spirit that stand's
>   by the naked man,
> in the booke of moones defend yee ...
>
> Of thirty bare years have I
> twice twenty bin enragèd,
>   & of forty bin
>   three tymes fifteene
> in durance soundlie cagèd,
>
> On the lordlie loftes of Bedlam
> with stubble softe & dainty,
>   brave braceletts strong,
>   sweet whips ding dong
> with wholsome hunger plenty ...

That is nonsense, too, but of a different kind from Lear's. This
superb poem of 'Tom o' Bedlam', of which hardly more than the
beginning is given above, has been made the subject of an entire
quarto monograph, in the impeccable scholarship of Jack Lindsay,
under the title *Loving Mad Tom*, published at the author's own
Fanfrolico Press in 1927 (which is getting to be the only way to do
things anymore), and giving samples of the endless variants rung,
in the same metre, throughout the seventeenth century, in praise
of tobacco, in dispraise of women, in mockery of the Puritans,
and for the benefit of other 'wandering professions' besides that
of madman: tinkers, blind beggars, jovial peddlars, oakermen,
and simple drunkards – a whole anthology of superlative balladry,
all in the limerick metre of 'Tom o' Bedlam'.

Later, in its turn, 'Tom o' Bedlam' also inspired the one greatest mad-song of the English language, 'Halloo my fancy', written in part (at the age of eighteen) by Col. William Cleland, uncle of the author of *Fanny Hill*. 'Halloo my fancy' is given complete, along with 'Tom o' Bedlam', in Charles Williams' and Lord David Cecil's *New Book of English Verse* (1935), pp. 419–24 and 249–51, where both will well repay the trouble of looking them up. The original text of 'Halloo my fancy' is in the *Percy Folio Manuscript*, about 1620 (edited by Hales and Furnival, 1868); and, as revised by Cleland, at the end of the first part of James Watson's *Choice Collection of Comic and Serious Scots Poems* (Edinburgh, 1706–11, repr. Glasgow 1869. A humorous imitation, called 'The Shiftless Student', has not formerly been noted: it appears in Sir John Mennis' and Dr. James Smith's *Wit and Drollery*, 1661, pp. 223–6.)

The one subject other than madness and rascalry for which the limerick metre was at first found utterly fitting was the praise of the much-censured tobacco, as first in the moralizing 'A Religious Use of taking Tobacco', or 'The Indian Weed', usually but erroneously attributed to Thomas Jenner or to George Wither, whose attack on smoking in *Abuses Stript and Whipt* (1613) seems – but only seems – to be recollected in its opening line:

> The Indian weed, witherèd quite,
> Green at morn, cut down at night,
>   Shows thy decay,
>   All flesh is hay:
> Thus think, then drink Tobacco.

(The full text will be found in Quiller-Couch's *Golden Pomp*, 1896, and his *Oxford Book of English Verse*, 1900, No. 390–*i*; also in William S. Braithwaite's very valuable *Book of Elizabethan Verse*, 1908, No. 522, noting its real author. It is printed exactly from MS. 877, Trinity College, Dublin, in Norman Ault's *Elizabethan Lyrics*, 2nd ed. 1928, pp. 53, 506.) The real author of this four-stanza moralization in the limerick metre was Robert Wisdome, a Protestant divine who died in 1568, having been a fugitive in Germany during the reign of Bloody Mary. 'The Indian Weed' was first printed without author's name as the last of the 'thirtie and one spirituall emblems' in Thomas Jenner's *The Soules Solace* (1626) f. G3*v*, and was much revised by a Scottish dissenting minister, Ralph Erskine over a century later – he died in 1752 – as

'Tobacco Spiritualised', beginning: 'Tobacco is an Indian weed', the form still sung today.

Inspired by Wisdome's 'Indian Weed', or perhaps its own folk source, is a solitary surviving limerick stanza, also in the iambic foot, 'O Metaphysical Tobacco', in *A Book of Madrigales for Viols and Voices* (1606):

> O metaphysical Tobacco,
> Fetched as far as from Morocco,
>   Thy searching fume
>   Exhales the rheum,
> O metaphysical Tobacco.

(Reprinted by Dr. Edmund H. Fellowes, *English Madrigal Verse*, 1920, p. 81, and first recognized as a limerick [by Richard Linn Edsall] in the *Atlantic Monthly*, Boston, 1924, vol. 134: p. 135.)

Still in transition towards the anapestic foot – here in the couplet only – and evidently drawing from 'Tom o' Bedlam' in its echoic chorus, the limerick form appears in print full-fledged in Barten Holyday's university comedy, *Technogamia, or The Marriages of the Arts* (1618) II. iii, but again either the first line does not rhyme, or the last is still a repeat:

> Tobacco's a Musician
> And in a Pipe delighteth:
>   It descends in a Close
>   Through the Organ of the nose
> With a Rellish that inviteth.

> *This makes me sing, So ho, hó –*
>   *So ho hó, boyes!*
> *Ho boyes, sound I loudly:*
>   *Earth ne're did breed*
>   *Such a Joviall weed*
> *Whereof to boast so proudly.*

In the same play, Act III, scene v, Holyday uses the limerick form in a love-song, humorously of course, as the impish but false 'beginna-a' rhyme shows:

> Come kisse, come kisse, my Corinna
> And still that sport wee'l beginn-a

That our soules so may meet
In our lippes, while they greet,
Come kisse, come kisse, my Corinna.

A love-song in limerick – the first, I believe – had already been
attempted at least a decade before, in Robert Jones' *The Muses
Gardin for Delights, or The Fift Booke of Ayres* (1610; the modern
reprint, Oxford, 1901, is expurgated of song No. 13, 'As I lay
lately in a dreame'). This is the first song in the book, the simple
and naïve 'Love is a pretty frenzy':

Love is a pretty pedlar
Whose pack is fraught with sorrows,
With doubts and fears
With sighs and tears,
Some joys – but those he borrows.

Even the use of the limerick as a chorus in drinking-songs was
seen in England about the 1610s, antedating by almost a century
the presumed use of such choruses in Limerick, Ireland. The
round-song, 'Now that the Spring hath filled our veins', by
William Browne (*fl.* 1614), a university poet of the school of
Spenser and Ben Jonson, not only has the rhyming couplet actually marked in stanza 2, 'Sing we a song with merry glee', but ends
in a limerick stanza – with anapestic couplet and conclusion –
sung in chorus by 'All'. (Printed in William S. Braithwaite's *Book
of Elizabethan Verse*, 1908, No. 36.) Note that the first line still
does not rhyme:

Shear sheep that have them, cry we still,
But see that nó man 'scape
To drink of the sherry,
That makes us so merry,
And plump as the lusty grape.

The necessary rhyming word at the end of the opening line of
the true limerick, calling forth all the matching rhymes, was also
achieved by the 1610s, as in Holyday's 'Corinna' song, and later
became standard at the popular or folk level of the broadside
ballads. For example, in 'The Two Yorkshire Lovers, A Pleasant
Northerne Song, To the tune of *Willy*' (before 1633; in *Roxburghe*

Ballads, ed. William Chappell, 1873, II. 228; the tune being identical with that of 'Tom o' Bedlam'):

> Of nuts Ile give thee plenty
> And red-side apples twenty:
>   My butter Ile lease
>   To make thee summer cheese,
> And creame to make egge-pies dainty.

Despite the charm and simplicity of the images and rhymes, the difficulty of being altogether serious in so rollicking a rhythm was clear almost from its beginning. Also, always in the background, was the sinister echo, the warning clack-dish or bell, of the original madmen and rascals whose song it was. Perhaps this explains why, as Jack Lindsay has wondered (*Loving Mad Tom*, p. 67), 'the possibilities of this insinuating stanza as a wooing poem were not much followed up'.

One last ghost to lay, or snake to scotch, before closing this consideration of the early proto-limericks of the Elizabethan age: Robert Swann and Frank Sidgwick, in *The Making of Verse* (1934), p. 101, first drew attention to the formal if somewhat tenuous relation between the limerick form and the 'short metre' or 'Poulter's measure' of Elizabethan hymnology. This is composed of two long lines, alternating twelve and fourteen syllables, and rhyming with each other in couplet form. It is usually divided, by pauses, into four lines of six, six, eight, and six syllables respectively, as in Shakespeare's *A Midsummer Night's Dream*, III.i.22, where Quince wants the Prologue to be 'written in eight and six'. There is no inner rhyme in the eight-syllable line, as would be necessary to make it into a short couplet, thus approaching the limerick form in a recognizable way. Swann and Sidgwick note several Elizabethan poets who used this 'short metre', p. 63, and give a stanza of this kind attributed to Queen Elizabeth:

> The Daughter of debate
> That eke discord doth sow,
> Shall reap no gain where former rule
> Hath taught still peace to grow.

Despite the long third line, of eight syllables, this is obviously not a limerick. Very curiously, however, a variant form of this stanza is quoted in Baring-Gould's *The Lure of the Limerick* (1967), pp. 15–16, on the authority of the modern poet Leonard Bacon, who maintains that Queen Elizabeth has here closely approached the limerick form 'by introducing the interior rhyme in the fourteen-syllable line'. Unfortunately, there is something very wrong with Queen Elizabeth's poem, as Mr. Bacon gives it. An interior rhyme has indeed been introduced, with numerous other changes, the second and third lines above now reading as follows:

> Who discord aye doth sow,
> Hath reaped no gain
> Where former *reign* . . .

What is most singular, perhaps, about this quotation, is that only and precisely this sixth stanza (of eight) is given, in changed form, that is quoted in its original form by Swann and Sidgwick. Nor is even the pretence made, concerning this brief poem by Queen Elizabeth, 'The Doubt' (given complete in William S. Braithwaite's *Book of Elizabethan Verse*, London, 1908, preceding No. 1), that any of the *other* seven stanzas, all in the same 'short metre', contain any internal rhyme at all! One wonders about the source of Mr. Bacon's text.

There is no authority whatever for this unavowed change of the non-rhyming 'rule' to the rhyming *reign*, on which the whole case for this, as a limerick, rests. It will be observed that the second line has also been grossly modernized: 'That' is changed to *Who*; also 'eke' to *aye*, and 'Shall' to *Hath* (changing the tense of the poem entirely). Worst of all, the changed position of the word '*dis*cord' seems intended to give it the modern pronunciation, with the accent on the first syllable, though it was pronounced by the Elizabethans – as the original text, above, makes clear – with the accent always on the last, as 'dis*cord*'. Verdict: the so-called limerick of Queen Elizabeth must be dismissed as a clumsy modern fake, by hand or hands unknown. In the same way, an accidental – or perhaps purposeful – inner rhyme in a similar Latin hymn attributed to St. Thomas Aquinas (*Thanksgiving after Mass*) has led eager searchers, of the type who write of their discoveries to the Sunday papers, to credit the Italian monk, Aquinas, with the creation of the English limerick. Again, to say the least, an error. (On this presumed discovery see the review by

the English limerick-poet, Father Ronald Knox, in *English Life*,
February 1925, of Langford's Reed's *The Complete Limerick
Book*. Also *New York Times*, 1 August 1944, p. 14/7.)

III

Formal poets have never scorned the possibilities of the madmen's
song and its limerick metre. On this pattern, Edgar, in Shakespeare's *King Lear*, III.iv.120, disguised as the mad beggar,
'poore Tom', chants his spell to the rhythm of 'Tom o' Bedlam',
and here there is no mistake about the couplet:

> Swithold footed thrice the old,
> He met the night mare and her nine fold,
> > Bid her alight
> > And her troth plight,
> And aroint thee, witch, aroint thee!

At least three other songs by Shakespeare are also in the limerick form: Iago's drinking-song in *Othello*, II.iii.70, which he states
he 'learned . . . in England, where indeed they are most potent in
potting', beginning: 'And let me the cannakin clinke, clinke'; and
Ophelia's touching mad-song in *Hamlet*, IV.v.190, 'And will he
not come home again?' especially the second stanza, 'His beard
was white as snow'. Also first seen in Shakespeare is the modern
rising anapestic metre of the limerick, replacing the older iambics,
as in Stephano's sea-song in *The Tempest* (MS. 1612) II.ii.52:

> For she had a tongue with a tang,
> > Would cry to a sailor, Goe hang!
> She lov'd not the savour of Tar nor of Pitch
> Yet a Tailor might scratch her where ere she did itch:
> > Then to Sea, Boyes, and let her goe hang!

This innovation of a double-length couplet was never followed
up, and is seldom used in modern limericks, Shakespeare himself
remarking: 'This is a scurvy tune too . . .'

As will be observed, two of Shakespeare's songs in the limerick
form are mad-songs, and two are drinking-songs; implying that
he felt the form was too 'popular' or too simple to be used
seriously. Yet the possibilities of the same metre, for 'pure' or

lyric poetry, were brilliantly explored by the rival school of Ben Jonson, first in Jonson's own 'Wheel of Fortune' song, 'The Faery beame uppon you', in his *Masque of The Gypsies Metamorphos'd* (MS. 1621; *Works*, ed. Herford and Simpson, 1941, VII. 573–5, lines 262–306).

There is a clear connection between Jonson's *Masque of The Gypsies Metamorphos'd* and Barten Holyday's play *Technogamia*, three years before. The limerick song in Holyday's play, in praise of tobacco, 'Tobacco's a Musician', quoted above, had offended tobacco-hating King James when the play was given before him late in August 1621. (See John Nichols, *Progresses . . . of King James I*, 1828, vol. IV (IIIb): p. 714; and Anthony à Wood, *Athenae Oxonienses*, 1692, II. 170.) At the third presentation of Jonson's masque before James, early in September of the same year at Windsor, lines were specially added by Jonson at the end of the 'Divells Arse-a-Peake' song (*causâ modestiae*, 'Cock-Lorell song') and elsewhere, obviously intended to contradict Holyday's encomium, and declaring tobacco to be the Devil's clyster-pipe and its odor his farting. (*Works*, ed. 1941, VII. 603, 610–11; lines 1126–37 and 1349–60.) Here is the opening of Jonson's 'Wheel of Fortune' song, in the 'Tom o' Bedlam' metre already used by Holyday, but with an extra inner rhyme in the couplet:

> The faery beame uppon you,
> The starres to glister on you,
> 　A Moone of light
> 　In the Noone of night
> Till the firedrake hath ore'gone you.

Unquestionably through Jonson, whose protégé he was, great ugly Robert Herrick was led to attempt a love-song in the limerick stanza, the exquisite 'Night-piece: To Julia', first published in his *Hesperides* in 1648, though undoubtedly written long before. That the very images here are improved from Jonson's gypsy 'Wheel of Fortune', just quoted, is remarked upon by Jack Lindsay (*Loving Mad Tom*, 1927, p. 66), and in Norman Ault's *Seventeenth Century Lyrics* (1928), p. 483. Herrick's 'Night-piece' begins superbly:

> Her eyes the Glow-worme lend thee,
> The Shooting starres attend thee,

And the Elves alsó
Whose little eyes glow
Like the sparks of fire, befriend thee.

No *Will-o'-th'-Wispe* mis-light thee,
Nor Snake, or Slow-worme bite thee:
But on, on thy way
Not making a stay,
Since Ghost there's none to affright thee.

The rest is not given here, to leave the pleasure and the discovery of this jewel, to whoever does not know it, who will look it up. (*Oxford Book of English Verse*, No. 262; and the original text in Herrick's *Poetical Works*, ed. F. W. Moorman, Oxford, 1915, p. 217.) It should be mentioned that the relation of both Jonson's 'Wheel of Fortune' and Herrick's 'Night-piece' to 'Tom o' Bedlam' was first noted by Miss Ethel Seaton in the *London Mercury* (1923) VIII. 79, to which journal is owed all the modern interest in Mad Tom's song, already in danger of being forgotten again, despite its rediscovery and reprinting, almost complete, at the article 'Tom o' Bedlams', in Isaac D'Israeli's *Curiosities of Literature* (ed. 1849, II. 343–9).

Very typical and personal in Herrick's poetry is his sado-masochistic alternation of character. On the one hand are his sweetly beautiful foot-and-breast-oriented love songs, not forgetting, however, the foot-and-underwear fetishism of the masochist ('Shew me thy feet', 'When as in silks my Julia goes', and 'The Description of a Woman', ed. Moorman, pp. 404–6), the concentration on the woman's body odors ('Love perfumes all parts' and 'Upon Julia's unlacing her self'), the frank references to cunnilinctus as a submissive act ('Pardon my trespasse, Sylvia', and 'Blisse, last night drunk'), and even to bondage and flagellation ('Bind me but to thee with thine haire' and 'Sufferance'; also throughout his religious *Noble Numbers*).

On the other hand are Herrick's endlessly bitter and sardonic epigrams, mixed in; modelled on those of Martial, and, like their model, revelling in sexual and scatological insult. Most of these are addressed to men – in sado-masochistic alternation or structuring referred to above – but the most violent of all, on the stalking horse or Turk's-head victim, the ugly old woman or frightful witch, is 'The Hagg', of which Herrick wrote two versions, one more ugly and scatological than the other. (*Poetical Works*, ed. Moorman, pp. 225 and 333–4.) See further, on the tradition of this anti-gallant alternation in the earlier French satirical poets, the 'Blasons' and 'Contreblasons' of the *fabliaux* period, and especially Robert Angot de l'Eperonnière in his *Euterpe, ou La Muse épineuse* (1637), in my *Rationale of the Dirty Joke: Second Series*, 14.1.4, the chapter 'Dysphemism, Cursing and Insults'. Shakespeare's alternating gallant and anti-gallant *Sonnets*, Nos. 127 and 130, 'My mistress' eyes are nothing like the sun', are also very much in this tradition – though comparatively mild. Predictably enough, the limerick rhythm of the lovely 'Night-piece: To Julia' is also adapted by Herrick to the crude anti-woman doggerel of his 'Upon Jone and Jane' (ed. Moorman, p. 229):

> *Jone* is a wench that's painted,
> *Jone* is a Girle that's tainted;
>   Yet *Jone* she goes
>   Like one of those
> Whom purity had Sainted.

> *Jane* is a Girle that's prittie,
> *Jane* is a wench that's wittie;
>   Yet, who would think
>   Her breath do's stinke,
> As so it doth? that's pittie.

Eventually, another friend of Ben Jonson's and member of his poetic school, Bishop Richard Corbet, removed the limerick rhythm almost completely from the use of madmen, lovers, and tobacco-addicts, to personal satire, as in Herrick's 'Upon Jone and Jane', somewhere in the early seventeenth century. Here, in satire, the limerick has principally remained. The surviving element of 'Tom o' Bedlam's' insanity is perhaps the concentration, still today, upon 'nonsense' in the clean limerick, of which Prof. Morris Bishop observes frankly (in the *New York Times Book Review*, 3 January 1965): 'The structure should be a rise from the commonplace reality of line one to logical madness in line five.' In other words, 'Tom o' Bedlam' rationalized but still in chains.

Bishop Corbet's famous limerick ballad, 'The Distracted Puritan', which was probably the most popular song of the English

Revolution – on the Royalist side – was written before 1636, but could only first be printed after the Restoration, at the end of the drollery-book *Le Prince d'Amour, or The Prince of Love* (1660); also in *The Rump* (ed. 1662) I. 237–9, as 'The Mad Zealot'. The Apocalyptic 'beast' referred to is, of course, Roman Catholicism:

> Of the beast's ten hornes (God bless us)
> I have knockt off three already:
>   If they let me alone
>   I will leave him none,
> But they say I am too heady.

> *Boldly I preach, Hate a Cross –*
>   *hate a Surplese!*
> *Miters, Copes and Rochets!*
>   *Come hear me pray*
>   *Nine times aday,*
> *And fill your heads with Crotchets.*

Corbet is adding here, to the galloping anapests of his stanzas, 'Tom o' Bedlam's' old refrain, with its strange pausing echo after the first line, to fit its melancholy tune, thus making melodically clear – as well as in words – the intended satirizing of the Puritan ranter as insane. Even the purported response to Corbet, 'The Zealous Puritan', written about 1639 but only first allowed to be printed in *Merry Drollery* (1661), replies in the identical metre. Corbet thus set the tone for all the later anti-Puritan and Restoration satire in limerick form, much of which is also insistently scatological in its humor.

All the drolleries, in fact, through to the last and largest of these, John Playford and Thomas Durfey's *Wit and Mirth, or Pills to Purge Melancholy*, in six volumes (1699–1720, and modern reprints), are absolute encyclopaedias of bawdy songs in the limerick metre, along with many other metres of course. Some continue the format of 'Tom o' Bedlam', but as to other trades, with the unmistakable pause-line in the whining refrain; others are simply in the satirical style of Herrick and Bishop Corbet (without refrains); and some curiously hark back to Holyday's 'Corinna', half a century earlier or more, which either had created a rhyming-style or had itself been set to a folk-tune (*'John Dory'*) with unaccented -*a* ending one or more lines. Even the briefest

examination of the drolleries will show that the concentration on
verbal obscenity and scatology, imagined by many to be a modern
addition to or perversion of the limerick form, is already in very
florid cultivation in the seventeenth-century drollery limericks, as
for example in 'Joane Easie', printed in *Wit and Drollery* (1661)
with an extra couplet and conclusion:

> Joane Easie got her a Nag and a Sledge
> To the Privy-house for to slide, a:
>   The hole was beshit
>   That she could not sit,
> But did cack as she lay on her side, a:
>
>   She was not wind [?]
>   For she sent forth a sound
> Did stretch her fundament wide, a.

So many examples of these evident predecessors of the modern
limerick, mostly in anapests mixed with the iambic foot, could be
quoted from the great outpouring of English humorous and folk
poetry in the seventeenth century, especially in the satirical
drollery collections of the Restoration, that one despairs of trying,
short of having the space of a whole book to quote them in. For
a very full, but by no means complete, selection, the reader is
referred again to Jack Lindsay's elegant monograph, *Loving Mad
Tom* (1927), with which one can disagree only as to the accus-
tomed balderdash of Mr. Robert Graves, in his Foreword; and
the excessive caution of Lindsay's inquiry (p. 75) whether it be
not 'fanciful to see something of a lingering memory or a chance
re-invention of the stanzaic effect in the limerick of our contemporary conversation, in which is crystallised so much brilliant
obscenity'.

IV

A particular element, which entered these early limericks at some
time during the seventeenth century, was the obviously satirical
use of proper names – of persons, later places – to set the opening
rhyme, or in other rhyming positions. To us, at least, these seem
intentionally burlesque, yet they were by no means always so
intended in that century. Herrick uses namerhymes often in his
humorous and sardonic epigrams, sometimes in the closing

couplet: always a prime doggerel position, as at the ends of the
Acts in Shakespeare's plays and those of his contemporaries. In
Herrick's 'Upon Jack and Jill' (ed. Moorman, p. 186), Jack feeds
Jill on kisses, telling her that these are the 'food of Poets', to
which she replies, obviously wanting something more solid:

> Let Poets feed on aire, or what they will;
> Let me feed full, till that I fart, says *Jill*.

In his 'The *Peter*-penny' (ed. Moorman, p. 256), in the two-
couplet metre of which the limerick form itself may be a worn-
down survival, Herrick end-rhymes not only on the Paternoster
('No pennie, no Pater Noster': an old proverb), but also boldly
rhymes 'St. Peter' with 'sweeter'! Even more outrageous to
modern ideas of formal poetry is the opening of Herrick's 'To
God', in his very serious *Noble Numbers* (1647; *Works*, ed.
Moorman, p. 343), involving not only a double rhyme on proper
names to open the poem, as will be seen, but even the diddley-
dumpty syllable-ing out of *Revela-ti-on* to make the needed five
syllables:

> Do with me, God! as Thou didst deal with *John*,
> (Who writ that heavenly *Revelation*).

Perfectly acceptable then, in the gravest kind of apostrophe to
God, a rhyme like that can be used today only in the most burlesque type of humorous poetry and song, for example the college-
girls' song about the tubercular prostitute: 'Lil, she was a beauty;
She lived in a house of ill repute-y', who finally has to drink
'Scott's Emul-si-on'. Altogether anti-clerical and anti-godlin, this
song is probably parodying an American survival of syllable-ing
out in singing hymns.

Barten Holyday's false-rhyme or added syllable, to rhyme with
the name, 'Come kisse, come kisse, my Corinna', in his play
Technogamia (1618) III. v, has already been quoted. By the time
of the English Revolution and Restoration, with their satirical
drollery-collections in verse, the use of proper names to open the
song or poem had become essential to the personal satire that was
the drolleries' stock-in-trade, even when a rhyme could not be
found. For example, in an anti-Puritan, anti-Cromwell song to
the old tune of 'Tom o' Bedlam', appearing in *The Rump, or*

*Collection of Songs and Ballads, made upon those who would be
a* Parliament, *and were but the* Rump *of an House of Commons,
five times dissolv'd* (1660: a hoked-up scatological title for a
drollery-book first issued in the same year as *Ratts Rhimed to
Death, or The Rump-Parliament Hang'd up in the Shambles*). This
is Sir John Denham's 'News from Colchester, or A Proper new
Ballad of certain Carnal passages betwixt a Quaker and a Colt',
demonstrating 'that a Mare's as good as a Madam' (ed. 1662)
I. 354 ff.:

> Help, Woodcock, Fox, and Naylor,
> For Brother Green's a Stallion:
> > Now alas what hope
> > Of converting the Pope
> When a Quaker turns *Italian!* . . .

(The Italians have always had a bad reputation, since Roman
times, for sexual perversion, especially anal intercourse. This is
nowadays usually assimilated to the even older Greeks.)

Two songs earlier in the same work – skipping over 'The four
Legg'd Elder; or a Relation of a Horrible Dog and an Elder's
Maid' – 'The Bloody Bed-roll, or Treason displayed in its Col-
ours' (ed. 1662, I. 343–50) entirely in double-limerick stanzas and
entirely of named personal satire, beginning: 'Old Oliver's gone
to the Dogs . . .'

> Here cómes Sir HENRY MARTYN
> As good as ever pist,
> > This wenching beast
> > Had Whores at least
> A thousand on his list.

Even the falsely stressed iambic opening, 'There *was* . . .' so
typical of modern limericks, was not uncommon in early seventeenth-century humorous verse, if not earlier, as in:

> There was a Lady lov'd a hogge, hony quoth shee,
> Woo't thou lie with me tonight? ogh, quoth he, *&c.*

Given thus, with the '*&c.*' implying a long folk-history preceding,
in an unpublished Twelfth Night revel, *Grobiana's Nuptialls*,
about 1620 (Bodley MS. 30). By 1 July 1626, a similar folk-
opening for a humorous poem or nursery rhyme was recorded:
'There was a Crow sate on a stone, He flew away and then there

was none' – the ancestor of the modern 'Ten Little Injuns' – in a satirical parody on the failure of the piratical expedition of the party of Buckingham against Cadiz, in Spain, in 1625, of which the failure left England bankrupt and the Revolution a certainty. (The song is quoted in a letter dated 1626, by the Rev. Joseph Mead of Cambridge; Harleian MS. 390. See further, on both the above, Iona and Peter Opie, *The Oxford Dictionary of Nursery Rhymes*, 1951, notes 294 and 355.) By the end of the seventeenth century, when the imitations by Samuel Butler and others in England of Scarron's travesties of the classics in France had made even anti-godlin and anti-Biblical 'mocks' and parodies a possibility, one had even such rhyme-openings as that in the invocation 'To the Reader', f. A7, in Samuel Colville's *Mock-Poem, or Whiggs Supplication* (1681): 'There was a Man called Job . . . He had a good gift of the Gob.' All of which leaves very little for modern limerick poets to invent.

Let me end this very brief survey, with one of the most technically unexceptionable seventeenth-century limericks, the first in which all the modern peculiarities of the form (with the exception of 'There *was*') appear: 'Mondayes Work . . . To the tune of *I owe my hostesse money*,' in the *Roxburghe Ballads* (ed. William Chappell, 1871–2) I. 514–20; II. 148–53. Published in broadside ballad form before 1640, this is a perfect modern limerick – anapestic metre (here and there), proper names setting the rhyme of the stanzas, and all:

> Good morrow, neighbour Gamble,
> Come let you and I goe ramble:
>   Last night I was shot
>   Through the braines with a pot
> And now my stomacke doth wamble . . .
>
> Gramarcy, neighbour Jinkin
> I see thou lovest no shrinking,
>   And I, for my part
>   From thee will not start:
> Come fill us a little more drinke in.

The rhyme here, as a matter of fact, is rather close to that of the modern bawdy limerick about the fellow named Perkin, whose gherkin was sherkin' his ferkin'; not to mention Skinner and

Tupper, who took the young lady to supper. A parallel inspiration or 'chance re-invention', to be sure.

Before another century had passed, the limerick form, now fully achieved in all its particulars, had so often been turned to the uses and abuses of satire, in poems and songs of drinking, wenching, and other 'low professions', that no one, not even Herrick, could have saved it as a lyric form, and Shakespeare's refusal to take it seriously was vindicated. Eventually the rhythm 'fell' – probably still carried by the wandering bedlam beggars, the ancestors of our own hoboes and tramps – to the dialect songs of Scotland and Ireland, as in 'Katy's Answer' to the young Laird, in Ramsay's *Tea-Table Miscellany* of 1724 (ed. 1871, I. 63):

> My mither's ay glowran o'er me,
> Tho' she did the same before me:
>   I canna get leave
>   To look to my loove,
> Or else she'll be like to devour me . . .

Certain of the peculiarities, picked up along the way, turned even the dialect form to dialect satire, particularly the use of a proper name (improperly, of course, according to the rules of all modern poetry but humorous) in calling forth the rhyme. 'Neighbour Jinkin', just noted, seems to deserve some part of the blame here, as the commonest tune used for the dialect satire songs in the limerick rhythm mentions him (in the anti-Welsh form of his name) in the opening line: 'Of noble race was Shenkin'. The same rhythm and tune are later used in a violently erotic piece, 'The Pious Parson', in all editions of *The Merry Muses* after 1830, still surviving in Britain as 'The Hero Alexander', referring not to the Macedonian emperor but to Alexander, Great Steward of Scotland, renowned for his heroism in the victory over King Haakon the Old of Norway, at the Battle of Largs in 1263. The surviving song is an adaptation of some of the anti-Puritan rhymes in 'The Bloody Bedroll', quoted above, now directed against either Protestant or Catholic clerics, depending on the singer's prejudices. Latest version, almost unexpurgated, in Harry Morgan's *Why Was He Born So Beautiful, and Other Rugby Songs* (London: Sphere Books – Nelson, 1967), p. 33, beginning: 'There was a priest, the dirty beast, Whose name was Alexander . . .' The hero of the Battle of Largs has been forgotten.

Finally, the limerick metre was abandoned altogether to the uses of nonsense and nursery rhymes – the classic decay and descent of much folklore, of which the last traces often survive only in children's rhymes and games. It is among the nursery rhymes, since the early eighteenth century at least, that the limerick form will mainly be found, as in 'Hickory dickory dock', 'Dance a baby, diddy', and many others that he who seeks will find. (See *passim* in Iona and Peter Opie's *Oxford Dictionary of Nursery Rhymes*, 1951, and William and Cecil Baring-Gould's *The Annotated Mother Goose*, New York: Clarkson N. Potter, Inc., 1962.) Quite in addition to those many eighteenth-century English nursery rhymes in classic limerick form, beginning 'There *was*...'

So typical of the nursery was the limerick with its rhyming on proper names eventually felt to be, that its form was used by mid-century in a mock-critical piece, 'To the Critics and Poets', reprinted in *The New Boghouse Miscellany, or A Companion for the Close-Stool* in 1761, p. 207, and burlesquing the pompous flatulence of the learned commentators of the day. This particular vein of satire had first been mined in Swift's *Tale of a Tub*, and Dr. William Wagstaffe's *Comment upon the History of Tom Thumb* in 1711, and by Hyacinthe Cordonnier, in his *Chef d'Œuvre d'un Inconnu* (1714) and its many imitations, which one would have thought had finished off the commentators and their excesses forever; but which are, instead, themselves forgotten, while the commentators go endlessly on.

The poem of the anonymous Boghouse poet is entitled –

On Jollity: An Ode, or Song, or both.

I

There was a jovial butcher,
He liv'd at Northern-fall-gate.
    He kept a stall
    At Leadenhall,
And got drunk at the boy at Aldgate.

II

He ran down Hounsditch reeling,
At Bedlam he was frighted,
    He in Moorfields
    Besh–t his heels
And at Hoxton he was wipèd.

The commentary that follows (by Oliver Goldsmith?) precisely in the mock-serious style later used by Norman Douglas in handling bawdy limericks, notes carefully, for example, how, in the second stanza, 'The geography of the places where the action happened is strictly observed.' This is almost identical with Douglas' note, as to the logical order of events in the equally scatological misadventure of the lady named Skinner (or Pinner), 'who dreamt that her lover was in her'. (Quoted at p. 241 below, Note 178.) It is also worth observing that, though proper names had already been set as rhymes in the limerick form, in 'Mondayes Work' – concerning neighbors Gamble and Jinkin – the present example, 'On Jollity', from the *New Boghouse Miscellany* of 1761, is the earliest 'geographical' limerick yet discovered (first appearing in *The Midwife, or Old Woman's Magazine*, about 1750, as reprinted also in *The Non-pareil*, 1757, pp. 165–70), and has certainly enough place-names, false rhymes, and even an opening 'There was . . .' to satisfy any historian.

v

So much for the history of the limerick before Lear, which has here obviously been only briefly sketched. Sufficient has been shown, however, to justify the opening statement that the limerick is, and was originally, an indecent verse-form. For anyone who cares to trace it further back than the unrepressed buckè of 'Sumer is i-cumen in', the field is wide open. But history, as everyone knows, is only half the story. The other half, and the harder part, is what is nowadays called the psychological element: earlier the 'soul', or spirit of the thing. Fortunately for any such profound study, all the materials are still in existence for the examination of the erotic content of the limerick, since its revival as a popular art form, and its elevation from the nursery, owing to the efforts of *Punch*, Lear, Leland, and the nameless poets of the 1860s.

All the materials, or perhaps lacking only one early document, chastely entitled *A New Book of Nonsense* (London, 1868), and extending to only twelve pages. This is the earliest collection of erotic limericks known to have existed, though no sure trace of this brochure has survived except a bare reference to its title, in the important Campbell-Reddie manuscript bibliography of nineteenth-century erotica (in the British Museum, II. 175). Almost immediately after, however, there appeared the much larger collection of bawdy and sacrilegious verse, *Cythera's Hymnal*, with the mock imprint 'Oxford: Printed at the University Press, for the Society for Promoting Useful Knowledge', 1870; which collection gives at the end a group of fifty-one erotic limericks, headed 'Nursery Rhymes', which, since they cover almost exactly an equivalent dozen pages, lead one to believe that the lost *New Book of Nonsense* of 1868 was perhaps only a pre-print of these pages.

Cythera's Hymnal is known, through the revelations of the bibliographer of erotica, H. Spencer Ashbee ('Pisanus Fraxi'), to have been the joint production of Capt. Edward Sellon, author of numerous erotic novels, and a study of Hindu eroticism, who died a suicide in 1866 (note the date); and the journalist, George Augustus Sala, assisted by several other Oxford men. The same authors also paid their respects to the classic erotic and satirical poet, Martial – their obvious inspiration, as he had been for Herrick – in an *Index Expurgatorius Martialis*, published at about the same time, and translating *only* those bawdy epigrams of Martial usually omitted from college pony-translations. Most of the poems of *Cythera's Hymnal* are howling and even revolting parodies, Sellon's 'Chordee' (a parody of 'Excelsior') being the least objectionable. From the viewpoint of the social critic, the most interesting piece is a satire on the noble do-gooders of the nineteenth century, out preaching a hypocritical gospel of sexual repression among the children of the poor. This is set to the infectious rhythm of the nursery rhyme or song, 'There was a little man, And he wooed a little maid, And he said, Little maid, will you wed, wed, wed?' printed for Walpole at the Strawberry Hill Press in 1764 as the work of Sir Charles Sedley, the Restoration wit.

This particular parody is reprinted, with a new group of sixty-five bawdy limericks spread through the eighteen consecutive issues, in the extraordinary erotic magazine, *The Pearl*, published secretly in London from July 1879 to December 1880 (with matching 'Christmas Annuals', which are very rare) by a mysterious individual of the real name of Lazenby – according to H. Spencer Ashbee's manuscript notes in the copies of his own bibliographies in the British Museum – using the obvious pseudonym of 'D. Cameron'. *The Pearl* has been reprinted complete at least four times, most recently – and for the first time openly – in New York by the Grove Press (1968) in one fat pocket-book. The parody referred to, entitled 'The Good Nobleman', is in the issue for August 1880 (Grove Press reprint, pp. 489–90), where it is perhaps worth looking up, as it is the funniest piece in the entire run of *The Pearl*, especially the penultimate stanza in which the disabused little children turn upon their hypocritical benefactor, and tear down his breeches to check on the purity he is preaching.

On the poetry side, and except for limericks, *The Pearl* is largely composed, like *Cythera's Hymnal*, of long narrative poems on flagellation, a type of sub-poetic doggerel excruciating for anyone to try to read who does not share this typically Anglo-Saxon and German perversion. Most of these poems may be suspected of coming from the pen of the journalist and war-correspondent, G. A. Sala, a man whose secret biography is waiting to be written. The hundred and twenty limericks included, in all, in these two sources, and in the continuations of *The Pearl* (and its 'Christmas Annuals') as *The Boudoir* and *The Cremorne*, falsely dated '1851', also include a large proportion of the bawdy limericks still in oral circulation in both England and America, and these must be considered the classics or old favorites of the genre. Evidently their main circulation, in both their own century and this, was by word of mouth, in the classic folklore fashion, and certainly not via the very rare secret publications, of limited circulation, in which they were committed to print.

I would not care to fall into the modern mania of counting and measuring the themes and motifs of the hundred and twenty limericks here cited, and the perhaps hundred and fifty more that make up the total 'float' or repertoire of orally-circulated modern limericks – the only ones that can be agreed to be socially indicative and significant. Much less would I care to try sliding them through the sucking-and-blowing apertures of a calculating machine, in order to discover the leading 'traits' or themes with which they are concerned, even assuming that anything meaningful could be learned in any such way. As the card-punching and sampling system has, so far, guessed wrong in all the political elections on which it has been tried, I do not think any serious folklorist would care to trust it with the significance of bawdy limericks.

Even without too much measuring, and Hollerith hole-punching machine entertainments, it is clear that, in a preponderant way, most bawdy limericks are concerned with the unconscious or unwilling *humor* of the sexual impulse: its organ-inferiorities, its attitudes and misadventures. The form being unrepressed, by definition, no holds seem to be barred as to the naked hostility expressed. The same is also true of clean limericks and of the even more sadistic 'Little Willies' proposed at the turn of the present century by Harry Graham ('Col. D. Streamer') in *Ruthless Rhymes for Heartless Homes*, first published in 1899, in a gleefully gruesome and anti-family style carried on for years afterwards – also in an attempted feminist version – by the murder-mystery writer, and clean limerick and whimsy-poesy fancier, Miss Carolyn Wells. All in all, a study of the quite unrepressed aggressions of the type of humor thought of as 'clean'.

The most gruesomely sadistic clean limericks are, of set purpose, those published as *The Listing Attic* (New York and Boston, 1954) and sequels, by a writer significantly named 'Edward Gorey'. Of 'Gorey's' productions, the by-no-means fainthearted critic, Clifton Fadiman, in his essay on limericks, 'There Was an Old Man of Tobago', in *Any Number Can Play* (Cleveland, 1957), remarks flatly: 'These are so appalling that I prefer not to quote them here. They are evidence of the bounds to which the Limerick may be pushed by an imagination at once febrile and cynical. Mr. Gorey thinks nothing of wrapping up such material as infanticide, simple murder, algolagnia, human vivisection, and the lynching of sexual deviants in a verse form traditionally consecrated to the innocent enjoyments of the nursery.'

It is curious how much of this sexual hostility in the frankly bawdy limericks is turned against the poet or protagonist himself, the hapless hero with whose disasters and phallic insufficiencies the limerick poet so clearly identifies. There can be no question that this is a sort of neurotic whistling in the dark, for the people who make up the bawdy limericks and who nowadays also sing them; attempting, as it were, to laugh away their sexual fears and impotencies – real and imaginary – in short satirical efforts of elaborate rhyme, in which, be it said once and for all, *woman* is the usual butt of the satire, as is true of almost all drinking songs.

The death of the limerick as a harmless if satirical verse form, in the early eighteenth century, was only a minor casualty in the broad campaign of moral repression, as well in literature as in ostensible life, operated in England at the level of printed matter by its early literary dictators, Alexander Pope, Joseph Addison, and the pachydermatous Dr. Samuel Johnson, the biggest literary bluff of his century. (There have been bigger since.) Quite aside from Johnson's English dictionary of 1755, expurgated into shape on the basis of Nathanael Bailey's earlier and *un*expurgated folio dictionary of the 1730s, under the flatulent Della Cruscan pretext of 'purifying' the English language – as though language depended upon dictionaries for its vocabulary! –, it should not be overlooked that Alexander Pope had already opened the battle with an expurgated edition of Shakespeare in 1725, though poor Dr. Bowdler, a century later, invariably gets the ridicule and the discredit. The bathetic depths of mock prudery to which the English-speaking world descended for two full centuries from the 1740s to the 1940s are too well known to discuss here, though there is little recognition of the hidden intention of shoring up economic privilege by these means against the advancing revolutionary spirit. This became extremely clear in the 'New Freedom' for both unrepressed speech and sexuality in the 1960s. (For an excellent introduction to the whole subject, see Victor F. Calverton's *Sex Expression in Literature*, 1926, a Marxist approach; Maurice Quinlan's *Victorian Prelude*, 1941; and Gordon Rattray Taylor's *The Angel-Makers*, 1958; as well as two excellent popular works, both entitled *Mrs. Grundy*, the first by Leo Markun, the second by Peter Fryer, 1963.)

As, in such campaigns for purity, sobriety, industriousness (note well!) and so forth, children and the working-class are the invariable first targets, the folksongs of the folk and the nursery rhymes of the nursery had immediately to go through the moral wringer. By the 1790s, with the 'clear and present danger' of the French Revolution escalating the moral war, even the outlying British territories, such as Scotland and Ireland – and, of course, America, by the usual cultural osmosis – were obliged to expurgate their folklore and folk-literature. This naturally led to the immediate creation of a subterranean erotic lore and literature, already begun in England under the moral suasions of the 1740s which had resulted at once i n the overblown Cytherean prose of John Cleland's *Fanny Hill* (1749).

That is how, and essentially that is why the limerick died, or rather was killed off, in the mid-eighteenth century. Already fallen away to the nursery and dialect level, it was laundered out of existence and disappeared. Thus, as was only to be expected, at its revival, just a century later, in the 1860s – taking off from the vapid innocuousness by then standard in the nursery forms, and in the imitations of these by Sharpe (1822), Lear, and *Punch* – the limerick, as revived, was somehow transmogrified by the poetry-loving nineteenth century, from mere 'nonsensical' bawdy and satire, into a gruelling combination of sick sex and sadistic scatology. And that is what the limerick now is. There are exceptions, of course: the healthy specimens or 'Little Romances from Real Life' with which the collection here presented begins; but, as their numbers show, they form only a very small minority. The limerick – the limerick really popular among adults – became a century ago, and still remains, the underground showcase and receptacle of all the most repellent erotic imaginings, the most scatological satire and aggression, and the sickest sexual fears and fantasies of the nineteenth and twentieth centuries, passed off always as *wit*, among the better-educated and presumably more cultivated classes. It is this record which is laid naked before the reader, at full length, in the collection which follows.

Far from being some victory for folk-poetry and unexpurgaiety, what had really happened was the inevitable and unhealthy result of the century-long censorship that both preceded and has run concurrently with the century of the bawdy limerick. The sexual censorship of the eighteenth century, and since, has operated always on a most significant principle or system of balances: the forbidding and removing of the sexual parts of literature and of life, no matter how normal; which assumes and involves that the necessary 'action' or excitement will then be supplied by the substitution of a permitted concentration on the most repulsive details of violence and death. As I have already published a hundred-page monograph on this cultural paradox or blind-spot that would make sex worse than murder, *Love & Death: A Study in Censorship* (New York: Breaking Point, 1949) – and the subject was in any case masterfully handled half a century before in

France, on the inspiration of a passage by Montaigne, in the eloquent diatribe, *The Pornography of Murder*, by Maurice Le Blond, the son-in-law of Zola – I will only touch upon it here.

One thing is certain: the Anglo-Saxon culture is now, and will long be harvesting the poisoned fruit of its demanded substitution of an allowed sadism for a prohibited sexual normality, despite the recent relative collapse of the censorship since 1960, first in the Scandinavian countries and now in America and England. The 'New Freedom' achieved is invariably accepted first, not as the long-awaited freedom from the censorship of sexual normality – which is its true purpose – but rather as an open social acceptance or shooting-permit for all the old degeneracies, such as sadism, sexual perversion, hallucinatory drugs, and the like, that every rational person was hoping to get rid of. The evil residue of the censorship is exactly this: that the new and partial literary freedom is immediately seized upon and exploited by the Gangsters of the New Freedom strictly as the freedom to print, propagandize for, and gloat over all the most nauseating details of the sadistic and other sex-linked abnormalities, which originally had appeared in literature and probably in life as an 'escape' from that censorship and its sexual repression.

The real point is not that the sex-substituted sadisms of modern literature, motion pictures, television, *and life* leap to any critical eye, but that the same substitution of an allowed sadism for the still-prohibited sexuality in the folk-literature and electrically-promulgated 'entertainment arts' of mass circulation in our time, can only result in the most dangerous and most sinister abnormalization of the whole psychic structure of future generations. That is the *real* message of the limericks of which the present collection is in major part composed, as it must be of any collection of authentic erotic folklore in the English language, sampled up out of the depths at the present time. As to the most recent social and human, rather than merely literary aspects of the same problem, see my pamphlet *The Fake Revolt, or Gangsters of the New Freedom* (1967), with its supplement, *Models of Madness*, specifically on the new drug 'scene' being peddled to adolescents. And if you can't read, look around and bear witness, brother!

VI

In the only serious psychological study ever made of limericks, by Prof. Weston LaBarre, in the journal *Psychiatry* (Washington, May 1939) II. 203–12, entitled 'The Psychopathology of Drinking Songs' but not quoting a single one, the important point is made that limericks are written and retailed only by the educated group, a group apparently perfectly attuned to the special impropriety of the limerick, both prosodic and moral. As the *Journal of American Folklore* was so kind as to allow me to remark a few years ago, in its epochal 'Symposium on Obscenity in Folklore' (July 1962, vol. 75: pp. 187–265), under the title 'Misconceptions in Erotic Folklore', an article reprinted in my volume of essays, *The Horn Book* (1964), without the expurgations demanded for the *Journal* symposium by a Dr. John Greenway – which came to half the total length of the piece! – bawdy limericks apparently represent for the educated group a sort of private revolt against the rules of prosody and propriety, at one and the same time, owing to the false accent with which most limericks begin, the improper geographical rhyme, and the gruellingly obscene subject-matter, which is usually of a far more alembicated nastiness than any other kind of folksong ever is.

This is a type of literary revolt that almost no other social class cares to share. Few persons of non-college background know, or want to know, any limericks at all, whether clean or bawdy, or perhaps only one or two used infrequently as toasts. Limericks are the folk-expression almost solely of the college group, particularly the professors, concentrating specifically on the bawdy limerick. The bawdy limerick remains thereafter the special delectation of college-educated men (and a few disoriented women nowadays), especially those in the quasi-intellectual professions, such as journalism, publishing, advertising, stock-jobbing, law and politics, and the entertainment arts. Limericks are not only the folklore almost solely of the educated, but are almost their *only* folklore, with the exception of jokes and tales – including a large number credulously believed to be true – and a limited repertoire of bawdy and sentimental songs remembered from college days.

Limericks are not liked by, nor commonly to be collected among, working men, farm-hands, cowboys, sailors, and other

classic oral sources – 'as yodelling tipplers are called by philolo-
gists' (Sydney Goodsir Smith). Many non-college and non-white-
collar people who have no objection to bawdry, will neither recite
limericks nor listen to them unless they are sung. Except for the
basic subject-matter, non-college people simply do not find it easy
to understand where the humor is supposed to reside, in all the
trick geographical rhyming and other purely formal and intellectual ornamentation of the limerick. It seems transpicuously clear
that the daring prosodic revolt of the falsely stressed 'There
was . . .' and the even falser geographical rhyme of the typical
limerick, do titillate persons who have been educated to believe
that these are poetically 'wrong', but no one else. The epigrammatic quality of the limerick, which it shares with its formal
ancestors of the *Greek Anthology* and the *Priapeia*, and among the
Roman satirists such as Martial, also makes it unsuitable for
non-college folk, who far prefer the larger developmental and
adventurous possibilities of the longer ballad form.

Since World War I and a bit earlier, an attempted democratiza-
tion has been taking place, in the possibility of *singing* the
limerick, in the eighteenth-century Irish style which apparently
gave the name of 'Limerick' to this verse-form. In Rudyard
Kipling's *Stalky & Co.* (1899), the story, 'The Propagation of
Knowledge' tells of singing-fests like this, with the chorus between stanzas, 'Won't you come up to Limerick?', among British
schoolboys as far back as about 1880. This tradition of singing
the limericks is obviously much more vital than declaiming or
reciting them, or simply collecting and trading examples in manuscript or typewritten form (now also on tape-recordings).
Limericks can now often be heard sung in the convivial company
of college fraternities (and sometimes sororities), the drinking-
clubs of army and air officers, and so forth; but even there the
groups involved are usually drawn from the educated classes.
Quite a number of limerick collections have in recent years been
mimeographed and privately circulated by such college and
armed-service groups, nothing 'new' ever appearing in these
mimeographica except the science-fiction limericks of recent vint-
age. The pages of limericks given are now clearly thought of as
a single object or song, with a chorus indicated.

As sung, the limericks are chanted *seriatim* by various members
of the group, to the tune, usually, of the venereal-disease song,

'The Spanish Nobilio' or 'Gay Caballero' (much worn down musically in the transmission), each singer electing himself or herself to come forward with a remembered or presumably extemporarily invented limerick, which thus becomes part of the 'song' being communally improvised by the group in classic folk-song fashion, and never twice the same. The stanzas are separated, and the singers allowed to catch breath, take a drink, or furbish up their inspiration, by a chorus or challenge sung by the whole audience:

> That . . . was . . . a very nice song,
> Sing us another one –
> Just like the other one –
> Sing us another one, do!

In America, the chorus or connective verse has become more recently, to the tune of 'Cielito lindo':

> Aye, yi, yi-yi! –
> In China they never eat chili;
> So sing me (here's to) the next verse,
> Much worse than the last verse,
> And waltz me around again, Willie!

In the courageous and competent *Annotated Field Collection of Songs from the American College Student Oral Tradition* – I guess that delimits the field very exactly – by Richard A. Reuss (Indiana University, Department of Folklore, master's dissertation, 1965), ff. 220–22, various burlesque versions or replies to the usual 'In China they never eat chili' line are cited, making a further possibility of extemporaneous elaboration between stanzas. Reuss cites: 'Freshmen never eat pussy . . .' and 'Your mother swims after troop ships . . .' also 'Your father licks toilet seats', which fails of the correct metre and is obviously only a catch-phrase of insult; with an even more elaborate form collected at Indiana in 1964:

> Aye, yi, yi, yi –
> I'd rather get laid than get eaten.
> So sing me a chorus
> While I eat your clitóris,
> So waltz me around again, Willie.

These have evidently come a long way from County Limerick. The intention here is openly to encourage the next singer to an even 'worse verse' – no longer merely 'another one, just like the other one' – as everyone becomes slightly more intoxicated, in part by singing, and a great deal less repressed. The British connecting chorus is the most interesting of all:

> Now hear, all ye dukes and ye duchesses,
>   Take heed of my warning, I say,
> Be sure that you owns all you touches-es,
>   Or I'll land you in Botany Bay!

These choruses are naturally sung in as many different ways as there are different singers, so it will be of no use writing to me in care of the publisher to say that the above wordings of the chorus are 'wrong', a word which has, after all, no real meaning folkloristically. One man's wit is another man's poison. Of course, additional *verses* in the limerick form would be far from unwelcome – as also songs and poems – but should perhaps be transmitted by homing-pigeon, St. Bernard dog, or some other uncommon carrier, as they might very well turn out to be illegal in the mails.

The note struck in the British limerick chorus, of absurd and out-of-place resistance to non-existent authority figures, such as the 'dukes and duchesses' who are boldly warned off the (sexual) property of the singer, is the crucial element in the psychological structure of all limericks, as in most erotic and satirical poetry whatever its metrical pattern may be. Authority figures can be almost anything or anyone, depending on the background of the poet or singer: some people hate royalty, some people hate bishops, monks and ministers, Englishmen or policemen. There are people who write books against the law of gravity (which they hate simply because it's referred to as a 'law'), or to prove that Einstein was wrong, or that Shakespeare was written *by another man of the same name*, as Mark Twain put it. I knew a man once who would become furious over printed signs in public places that did not begin with the word 'Please. . . .' Few people can admit that they are fighting non-existent authority figures, as they seldom fought the parents who are the real authority figures that they are still seething about, and who, in the present case, appear in the limericks they write or quote disguised as kings, dukes, and bishops.

The main focus of resistance and hostility in limericks tends to circulate in this way about perfectly mythical figures of royalty and nobility, such as the petrified image of poor mad George III hidden in American folklore since 1776 under the stereotyped heading of the hated Englishman or superior snob. See the entire section, 'Bloody Englishmen', in the chapter on Fools in my *Rationale of the Dirty Joke: First Series* (1968) pp. 167–71, which takes the whole matter a good deal further.

Resistance to the clergy comes only second in limericks, and would probably long since have faded, along with the now utterly uninteresting religious controversies stirred up a century ago by Darwin on evolution and Bishop Colenso's 'Higher Criticism' of the Bible, demonstrating that it is largely a forgery and could not possibly have been written by Moses. However, the geographical necessities of the limerick rhyme have perpetuated in certain favorite limericks such otherwise unknown and irrelevant dignitaries as the Bishops of Twickenham, Woking, and Chichester, of whom the last is practically dragged in by the seat of his britches only in order to get another part of that garment somehow involved in a florid rhyming scheme concerning a young lady whose charms had already 'made all the saints in their niches stir'. It is obvious that the ordinary cowboy, miner, field-hand or workingman will not go for effete and over-intellectual stuff like that.

The average working man, in such a mood, much prefers singing 'The One-Eyed Riley' or ' 'Twas on the Good Ship *Venus*' or 'The Bastard King of England' or 'The Crab Fish', when he does any singing at all, or is *allowed* to sing – even polite songs – in his public bar (where the juke-box or television machine suffers from no such restriction). Whatever he may sing in the way of bawdy, the uneducated singer inevitably prefers the more active and adventurous ballad form, giving room for a more phallic, and less pettily linguistic, sexuality.

Probably the pettiest of all revolts in the limerick is its intense concentration on the personal or geographical name setting the rhyme in the opening line. This is a leftover nursery-rhyme or satirical form of the early seventeenth century, as has already been shown. At best, it is a type of trick-rhyming – often triple: rhyming three full syllables in improbable fashion – splendidly done by certain nineteenth-century humorous poets like R. H. Barham in his *Ingoldsby Legends* (1837), Thackeray, Sydney Smith, and W.S. Gilbert; also in many limericks of the Golden Period, such as No. 1 in the present collection, usually attributed to Swinburne. It is a trick that palls rapidly unless very well done indeed, as implied in W. S. Gilbert's totally *non*-rhyming reply to Lear, on the old man of St. Bees, 'Who was stung in the arm by a Wasp'. (He thought it was a hornet.)

Another type of resistance is expressed in the infrequent mock-limericks in which, like the Young Man of Japan, 'You try to get as many words into the last line as you possibly can!' Langford Reed's *Complete Limerick Book* (2nd ed. 1926, p. 47) gives a more logical form of this, under the 'Clerical Limerick', supplied by Dean William Inge, with the last line – to rhyme with 'lamb' and 'jam' – 'We all heard our Vicar say, "Stand up please, while I say grace".' In Martin Gardner's edition of C. C. Bombaugh's *Oddities and Curiosities of Words* (New York: Dover, 1961), p. 362, the opposite is tried, concerning the Young Poet in China: 'His limericks tend, To come to an end – Quite suddenly.' As can be seen, all these new niceties are simply forms of revolt against the prosodic revolt that the limerick itself is supposed to be!

The principal attractiveness of personal or geographical rhyme in run-of-the-mill limericks, which often have not even the necessary excuse of personal satire, seems to operate solely on over-educated people, titillated by the idea that such rhymes are prosodically 'wrong', and therefore an expression of some private poetic revolt. Actually, in the seventeenth century, when the limerick assumed its modern form in all essentials, such rhyming was not only not considered wrong, but was even taken calmly to such lengths as the example already quoted from Herrick's apostrophe 'To God', in his *Noble Numbers, or Pious Pieces* (1647), which opens flatly with the absolutely howling rhyme of the name 'John' (the Evangelist) with *Revela-ti-on*! The total rejection of this concern with silly nominal rhymes in the limerick, by the author of some of the best modern erotic limericks, the late Carlyle Ferren MacIntyre, beginning with the famous 'While Titian was mixing rose-madder . . .' (No. 757, vol. II), which demotes the name-rhyme to the couplet, will be discussed further, at the end of this essay.

VII

Conscious of being without real audience over the last long century, practitioners of the 'clean' limerick have tried desperately for interesting minor innovations in the limerick form itself. Most of these presumed innovations are, however, mere petty peculiarities, amusing only to the most infantile and word-oriented minds. It should be observed, of course, that such infantile minds are particularly common in the principal haunts of the limerick: the faculties of language-study and mathematics in the university world, and the shady edges of intellectual pursuit, such as journalism, where what is dealt with is always strictly the external *form* or vehicle of ideas, never the true matter or *subject*, this being falsified or forbidden – like that crime against the Holy Ghost: expressing VALUE JUDGMENTS! – by the rules of these delayed-adolescent professions themselves.

Among the worst limerick innovations attempted have been, certainly, the hypothetically amusing re-spelling of the end words of the lines to match curiously pronounced English place-names, a type of vaudeville-stage humor dating from the 1900s in *Punch* and principally amusing to big-city hicks. All the whimsical humor of the resultant limerick-objects – which plainly admit that they aspire to no other humor – is presumed to rise from such kittenishness as bringing onstage a hero named Cholmondeley, pronounced 'Chumly', to rhyme with 'bumly' (spelled *bolmondeley*, of course); or Salisbury, pronounced 'Sarum', to rhyme with *halisbury-scalisbury*; or Featherstonehaugh, pronounced 'Fanshaw', to rhyme with 'handsaw' (spelled *handerstonehaugh*!); or perhaps Hampshire, pronounced 'Hants', to rhyme with *pampshire* for 'pants'. Very naughty, that. Out of mercy for the reader, I omit further examples.

Also purely verbal or literal in nature is the intended humor of the heavily assonant or alliterative style afflicted in Conrad Aiken's *A Seizure of Limericks* (1964):

> The limerick's, admitted, a verse form:
> A terse form: a curse form: a hearse form.
>   It may not be lyric
>   And at best it's Satyric,
> And a whale of a tail in perverse form.

So extreme a reliance on inner-rhyme or alliteration is typical of much ancient poetry, written during the infancy of any language, and is best seen in early English and Scottish alliterative verse. I have quoted one fine example of this in *The Horn Book*, p . 147, noting also its use in Urquhart's translation of Rabelais, and in the great Scottish 'Flyting' in insults – so similar to the modern Negro 'playing the Dozens' – between Polwart and Montgomery. The original, which is extremely long and obscene, will be found in James Watson's *Choice Collection of Comic & Serious Scots Poems* (Edinburgh, 1706–11; repr. Glasgow, 1869, III. 1–32), running to hundreds of alliterative lines.

Mr. Aiken's *Seizure of Limericks* is not derived from this type of authentic folk-source, but is apparently in imitation of similar verbal tricks and the semi-insane – or perhaps entirely insane – echolalic traits in James Joyce's *Finnegans Wake* and *Ulysses* (1922), earlier imitated *in toto* in Aiken's *Blue Voyage* (1927). Prof. Morris Bishop, who is himself a notable limerick poet in both the clean and semi-bawdy forms – I will not say more: these last in his murder-mystery *The Widening Stain* (1942), under the pseudonym, 'W. Bolingbroke Johnson' – has reviewed Aiken's *Seizure* slashingly in what is one of the most penetrating articles written 'On the Limerick' (in the *New York Times Book Review*, 3 January 1965), remarking icily on Aiken's title: '*Seizure* is good; a mild taste for limericks can lead to seizures, addiction, septic logorrhea and compulsive recitation neuroses.'

Other pathetically uninteresting peculiarities in modern limericks are evident attempts to jazz up the creaking machinery of the 'clean' variety and give it a new lease on life: attempts which have invariably failed. In particular, there is the omission of the last line, in puzzle style, which the reader is then challenged to invent. (*Line-lost Limericks*, 1915, by Fred E. Woodward.) This is the format of practically all the advertising contests based on limericks, in which, of course, as the present essay began by maintaining, the real and entire interest to everyone concerned is never the tons of worthless limericks fomented by these means, but the monetary prize or bait. Also attempting to import a bit of puzzle or mystery – replacing, unquestionably, the primitive sexual mystery being evaded in the clean limerick: '*Where do babies come from?*' – are the self-styled 'Glimericks, or Mystifying Limericks' proposed in the volume, *The Glimerick Book* (New York, 1925), credited to one 'Shaemas J. A. Witherspoon', believed to be the journalist Herbert Bayard Swope, editor of the *New York World*. In the mystery line there are even *Fifty Original Cryptogram Limericks* (1929) by George W. Wilson. But why go on? The real danger is that some machine-tending geek will realize that computing machines could easily be programmed to produce clean or bawdy limericks by the mile or until turned off, at which point we had all better leave for the Moon. (Compare 'The Sorcerer's Apprentice', and 'The Quern, or Salt-Grinding Mill': Aarne-Thompson folktale types Nos. 325* and 565.)

More interesting, certainly, is the double-couplet limerick, in which the couplet is extended to double length. As noted, this was invented – and immediately dropped – by Shakespeare, in *The Tempest* (MS. 1612), II.ii.52, in the song 'For she had a tongue with a tang', quoted above. Only the modern poet and stylist, Walter de la Mare, whose little-known short story, 'The Tree', is perhaps the most perfect gem of modern lapidary style, has attempted anything in the double-couplet line. These he calls 'Twiners', and presents two batches of them in his volume of humorous verse, *Stuff and Nonsense* (London, 1927). De la Mare's 'Twiners' invariably involve a sort of sub-sexual marriage arranged between two theoretically separate limericks, each with its own personal or geographical rhyme, one about a man and one about a woman. Their marriage is then consummated in verse, by alternating or intertwining line with line, including a couplet of double length or longer, as in his 'The Eel' (p. 54), of which the symbolic element is only too obvious:

> There was an old person of Dover
> Who called on his sister in Deal,
> With a sack hanging over his shoulder
> In which was a whopping great eel.
> It leapt down the area, scuttled upstairs,
> It golloped up bolsters and wash-jugs and chairs,
> Her boots, shoes, and slippers, in singles and pairs . . .

It ends, of course, with the ogresome Eel eating up the sister completely. Though both Shakespeare's and De la Mare's doubled anapests do make a rollicking rhyme, most limerick poets would probably find the 'Twiner' just as unsatisfactory a verse-form as it is patently a repressed sexual act or intermingling.

Only Ambrose Bierce, the best of the American turn-of-the-century 'black humorists', was able to infuse any real life into the doubled limerick form, but, in the form he proposed, it is precisely the couplet that remains – like its author-hero – irresolutely single. I quote the only example of Bierce's double-line limericks known to me, 'The Owl', from Wilson Follett's *Modern American Usage*, edited by Jacques Barzun (New York, 1966), p. 360, where it is intended to illustrate the boldly colloquial ungrammaticality of saying 'who', where petty grammarians and phoneme-grinders would demand 'whom':

> Sitting singly in the gloaming and no longer two and two,
> As unwilling to be wedded as unpractised how to woo;
> With regard to being mated
> Asking still with aggravated
> Ungrammatical acerbity: 'To who? To who?'

This compares well with the rapid pace of some of the best of W. S. Gilbert's patter-songs in the Gilbert and Sullivan operettas, several of which songs are purposely in limericks, as quoted by William Baring-Gould, *The Lure of the Limerick* (1967), p. 55. Baring-Gould does not correctly distinguish, however, pp. 15 and 54, between true modern limericks in the anapestic metre, and those longer ballads in the more rapid beat called the *paeonic* measure, an ancient Greek metre used for songs of joy or triumph (paeans), in a foot of four syllables – three short, and one long – in which, for example, 'The Story of Prince Agib', in Gilbert's *Bab Ballads* (1869) is cast. H. I. Brock's *Little Book of Limerick's* (1947) also quotes as a limerick a stanza in this metre, from the well-known lying-song of the 1900s, 'I Was Born About Ten Thousand Years Ago', of which there is also a recent political version called 'Passing Through' and a picketing parody, 'Pass 'em By!'. It should be recognized that these are all developed from the 'Pratie Song' of the Irish potato-famine of the mid-nineteenth century, which resulted in the Irish immigration to North America. Entitled 'The Wonderful Song of "Over There" ' (four stanzas, with music), this was first published by Atwill in New York in 1844. But compare the more honest yearning for Ireland – and to hell with 'North Ameri-kee'! – in the well-known parody of Allan Cunningham's 'Home, Boys, Home'.

Three further parodies or developments of the 'Pratie Song' are given in the present collection, pp. 177–80, No. 845 ff. Vol. II: 'Up at Yale,' 'Over There,' and 'In Mobile' (or 'On the Teal'), with a single-stanza song or recitation in the same metre, at No. 104, 'It's Only Human Nature, After All', in which the couplet is purposely spun out to double length – or *ad lib.* – all in rhymes on '-tion', to increase the mounting tension and orgasmic impact of the final mock-moralizing title line. These *paeonic* ballads are probably not really limericks at all, but are included in the present collection owing to their related erotic themes, and their use of so close a variant of the form. Again, it is curious that the line of descent leads back to Ireland, as with the intermediate limericks of the eighteenth century.

As a number of writings on the limerick, for example the introduction to the erotic collection by 'John Falmouth', *Ninety-five Limericks* (Suffern, N.Y., 1932), erroneously state that the limerick is in the dactylic metre, it is perhaps worth insisting here that the limerick is *not* dactylic, but anapestic. As these two different prosodic feet, which are the exact reverse of each other, both contain one long and two short syllables, the difference may seem unimportant, but it is actually of the very essence. The feel or *movement* of any song or poem in triple-metre is almost entirely determined by whether it RISES from its short syllables to an accented long syllable, or FALLS from its long syllable to the unaccented short. (On this very important point, see further Swann and Sidgwick, pp. 29–31.) The limerick, technically described, is in *anapestic trimeter*.

It is the anapestic short syllables that open the limerick line – one short syllable usually being dropped at the very beginning – and not the dactylic reverse. It is this that makes all the liveliness and bounce of the limerick form. A line of dactyls, to the contrary, almost invariably sinks continuously in dirge-like solemnity, striking hammer-hard at every foot. One has only to compare the joyous, rising gallop of that greatest of all anapestic passages, Rossini's *William Tell Overture* ('Titty-RUMP, titty-RUMP, titty-rump-rump-RUMP!') with the ever-descending gloom of the only long poem in English entirely in unrelieved dactyls, Thomas Hood's 'The Bridge of Sighs', so lugubrious that it is funny, beginning: 'One more Unfortunate, weary of breath, Rashly importunate, gone to her death'; and sinking to lines of such utter

dactylic bathos as: 'Ere her limbs frigidly, Stiffen too rigidly . . .'
(Oh, come *on*!)

> WHAT is the LIMErick's TRUE physioGnomy?
>   DActyl or ANapest, WHICH can it BE? –
> MErciful GOD how the DACtyl treads HEAVily . . .
>   While the ANapest GALlops with GLEE!

VIII

One of the elements in the limerick that has tended to further its
formalized presentation in private drinking-clubs, in the colleges
and elsewhere, is the greater ease of its recollection, in quintain
form, than that of the long ballads preferred by folksingers. This
epigrammatic or witty quality is common, as well, to the similar
form popular among German students, the 'Frau Wirtin' quin-
tains, and the erotic quatrains or 'Vierzeiler' of even wider popularity in the German-speaking countries. (See the collections in
E. K. Blümml's *Futilitates, Erotische Volkslieder*, and *Der Spittel-
berg*, Vienna, 1907–8, 5 vols., and 1924.) The historical original of
this formalized presentation is the erotic toast, about which little
if anything has ever been written. This type of toast – 'Gentlemen,
I give you (*or*, Here's to) . . .' followed by some prose or rhymed
typification of the person or institution to be drunk to by all – had
its greatest development in the mug-house clubs of Great Britain
throughout the eighteenth century. Various collections of these
toasts will be found printed in the erotic songsters and jestbooks
of the time, continuing well into the nineteenth century in all the
editions (except the first) of *The Merry Muses*. The toast is now
almost extinct in England, being reduced to the mere muttered
formula, 'Cheers!' to the fractured-English 'Chin-chin!' in
France, and the curious 'Mud in your eye!' in America, a scatological or equestrian survival. Much more will be found as to
erotic toasts, as survivals of earlier sexual *ordeals*, such as those of
mad lovers, in the draft of the present essay appearing in my *The
Horn Book* (1964), pp. 441–5, and, at quite a different level of
interpretation, in the section 'Cunnilinctus and Masochism', in
Rationale of the Dirty Joke: First Series (1968), pp. 573–5, to
which the interested reader is referred.

One of the clearest deficiencies of the limerick, preventing it
from ever achieving broad folk-acceptance, and keeping it class-

linked to the basically non-singing educated group, is the lack of a really good limerick tune. Almost anything is acceptable in the way of words, to both singers and audiences alike – though obviously not to poets – if the tune makes some basic appeal. If proof were required of this, one need only consider the unconscionable drivel set as words nowadays to so-called 'popular' songs, whose popularity is shorter-lived than a sick pup, in part because the tunes are so awful too.

The limerick has nothing to compare with the folksongs, as to music, and simple cannot compete. The 'Gay Caballero' tune, generally used, is hopelessly weak, and melodically very circumscribed. It takes quite a deal of alcohol to be able to listen to twenty limericks in succession sung to its tune, no matter how loud the audience shouts out the connecting chorus, and begs for 'another one'. The few efforts that have been made to work up a new limerick tune have never been followed, mostly because they are not worth following; for instance that attempted in W. R. Titterton's over-manly *Drinking Songs* (1928), which is also outfitted with a *tooralooloo* refrain, and an echoic repeat of the final line ('Please don't shoot the pianist – he is doing his best').

By far the best limerick tunes are those of Sir Arthur Sullivan, who – for a change! – dropped his cynical plagiarizing of Mozart and Offenbach (even his setting of the Rev. Baring-Gould's hymn, 'Onward Christian Soldiers' is nothing but the opening of Beethoven's *Violin Concerto*), and belted out at least three splendid limerick tunes: 'A man who would woo a fair maid', in *The Yeomen of the Guard* (1888); 'A plague on this vagary', in *Iolanthe*; also, in *Patience*, 'I shall, with cultured taste'; and especially that in *The Sorcerer* (1877), for the sorcerer's limerick song, beginning, 'My name is John Wellington Wells'. But this too has never been used, outside the Gilbert and Sullivan operetta. Its only influence seems to have been on the late Aleister Crowley, who luxuriated in the reputation of being 'the worst man in the world' – an undeserved distinction which he did his best to keep going by writing obscene and insulting limericks against all his friends, among other entertainments. Among the last that Crowley ever wrote is this poetic 'signature', parodied directly from Gilbert, but given here because it indicates the correct pronunciation of Crowley's own name, which people usually get wrong, while claiming nevertheless to have gone on Black Masses with him (in their youth):

My name it is Aleister Crowley,
I'm a master of Magick unholy,
Of philtres and pentacles,
Covens, conventicles;
Of basil, nepenthe, and moly.

A few of Crowley's bawdy limericks are given in his very rare volume of horrible parodies and pornographica, *Snowdrops from a Curate's Garden* ('Cosmopoli, 1881' [actually Paris, about 1904], copy: B.N. *Enfer*), at the end of the section, 'The Bromo Book', pp. 129–31. At least fifty others are extant, though still unprinted. Among them, another group of seventeen horrendous limericks by Crowley, almost all about intercourse with birds, is noted frankly at the end: 'Above all written straight off under the influence of cocaine in the early hours of the morning on 11 October 1920, at the Villa Santa Barbara, Cefalu, Sicily', with the penultimate note: '6.15 a.m. I'll shave.' They say that narcissistic details like this show the inner workings of a poet's mind, but I wonder.

The final question as to the limerick is that implied in Crowley's signed example: who are the authors of bawdy limericks? It is understood that most limericks entertain only their authors, and, whatever attempts may be made to circulate them, never achieve folklore status at all. But what of the others, that everyone knows – who writes them? Some of the original authors, when the form was new, and classics were being cast in the hot mould of Victorian anti-clericalism, have been mentioned above, in particular Swinburne, to whom what must be Limerick No. 1 in any collection has always been ascribed, the charmingly normal idyll, in extravagant rhyme, as to the young couple of Aberystwyth, 'who united the organs they kissed with', moving on finally – in lay-analytic terms – from the oral to the genital stage at last. Other known limerick authors of Swinburne's time and circle were Dante Gabriel Rossetti (who obviously had to write them, if only to get the 'languid love for lilies' of his published poetry out of his system), and the university humorist, A. C. Hilton, whose parody of Swinburne, 'The Octopus', is the funniest and most lethal example of the parodist's art in English. Of course, *which* limericks were written by which poets is the part most difficult to discover.

On the other hand, one is wise not to be taken in by the facile attributions of everything bawdy to everyone temporarily in the news. Nothing is sadder than to see the hoary attributions of bawdy folksongs to poets who never in the world wrote them, especially Lord Byron, changing faithlessly to new and equally positive attributions, as new writers come into vogue; these also soon to be replaced in their turn by others as the 'secret authors'. Thus one has recently seen Sala's bawdy farce, *Harlequin Prince Cherrytop* attributed in print to Gilbert and Sullivan (!) under the title *The Sod's Opera*, by the irrepressible Mr. Ralph Ginzburg, on the authority of a British barrister, Mr. St. John-Stevas, who should have known better (see the horrible details in my *The Horn Book*, pp. 95–6); and 'The Bastard King of England', which once used to be fathered off on Kipling – never forgetting to add, 'Yes, and it cost 'im the poet-lariatship too!' – later attributed to Robert W. Service, the sourdough poet of the Alaska gold-rush; then to A. P. Herbert, Member of Parliament; and, most recently – perish the thought! – to Noël Coward. It is the same with attributions of bawdy limericks to Tennyson, Woodrow Wilson, and who-not: one must ask to see the documentary proofs, or to speak to the person who is supposed to have heard the putative poet recite his verse. Or else, as with the great Sea Monster of Loch Ness, the case must be left 'unproved'.

Occasionally the matter is entirely reversed. *Everybody* wants to be the father, and instead of being unable to discover the author, one is embarrassed with an excessive richness of rival claimants. Of one particular item, probably of the 1930s,

> Have you heard about Magda Lupescu,
> Who came to Rumania's rescue?
> 　It's a wonderful thing
> 　To be under a king –
> Is democracy better, I esk you?

it is necessary sadly to admit that the present writer has personally encountered not one, but three separate and distinct 'authors' of this rhyme, one of whom – of Teutonic origin and fresh off the boat – could hardly pronounce any further words of the English language than this one limerick and his claim to authorship.

The bawdy limerick has now quieted down a good deal, from the days when it was an outcast thing, as evidenced in the remarkable letter on the mystery of its *name*, written by Dr. Murray, editor of the *Oxford English Dictionary*, to *Notes & Queries* in 1898, strongly objecting to its use in referring to innocent nonsense rhymes. It may be observed, as to the name 'limerick', that the bawdy examples in *Cythera's Hymnal* and *The Pearl*, in the 1870s, and finally in *The Cremorne* ('1851', really 1882), are invariably given under the rubric of 'Nursery Rhymes'. This pinpoints the coinage or acceptance of the name 'limerick' as at some time between 1882 and 1898, possibly in the columns of the sporting newspaper, *The Pink 'Un* (a sort of British *Police Gazette*; both being imitations of earlier French risqué journals on colored pulp, such as *Le Piron*), to which Murray's indignant letter seems to allude, if not to *Pick-Me-Up*, or *Judy*. A retrospective volume of *Purple Plums Picked from the 'Pink 'Un'* – of which the true title was actually *The Sporting Times*, founded in 1865 – was privately issued on the demise of this lively rag in 1931, on pink paper of course. Unfortunately, the 'Plums' reprinted cover only the period beginning with World War I. Among these are indeed included many slightly off-color limericks, which is probably about as naughty as *The Pink 'Un* ever got.

IX

The shelving away of the bawdy limerick now, almost as classic, is largely due to the collection published in Florence in 1928 by the Scottish antiquarian and novelist, Norman Douglas, who is the only person ever to have had the courage to sign a wholly bawdy limerick collection with his real name. *Some Limericks*, as Douglas' volume is modestly called, is not particularly large, containing only sixty-eight limericks, of which few can have been original with him, though one may suspect his improving hand in many. In his introduction, which is a masterpiece of dry humor, Douglas seems seriously to imply that he had also made a collection of Florentine swear words – and had 'caught the old ones in the nick of time' – at the period when he was also compiling the 'breathless catalogue' of his classic study (which he had to publish himself) of *London Street Games*, in 1913–16, with their titles so reminiscent of the similar list of old dances in the rediscovered manuscript fragments of Rabelais' *Pantagruel*, Bk. v, ch. xxxiii (translated by W. F. Smith, and Samuel Putnam). If the collection of swear words was not just one of Douglas' leg-pulls, which it does not seem to have been, it is a great pity it has not survived. Julian Sharman's perfectly titled *Cursory History of Swearing* (1884) does exist, and a more recent study by Prof. Burges Johnson, along with a curious manuscript collection on the subject, preserved at Princeton; and, for French, Robert Edouard's *Dictionnaire des Injures* (Paris: Tchou, 1967), with a similar work in Italian about ten years before; but these are not worth what a study at the hands of a master like Douglas would have been, as evidenced by the brief sample of his intended introduction, printed in that of *Some Limericks*.

If sheer size were any criterion, Douglas' work might be far overshadowed – which it most certainly is not – by the present collection, *The Limerick*, first published anonymously in Paris, 1953, giving nearly eighteen hundred bawdy limericks, good, bad, and indifferent, without critical evaluation or psychological study, but with a certain amount of historical annotation and folklore parallels. This reprints all formerly published bawdy limericks, and more than double that number of unpublished examples, arriving at the largest collection of limericks ever published, erotic or otherwise. An Addenda of nearly the same number of further examples has been accumulated since that time, in part from the private mimeographica of college students in the United States, and other privately printed works, and this should eventually be published. Meanwhile, a pamphlet plagiarism – if folklore can ever be said to be plagiarized – was issued by Maurice Girodias-Kahane's Olympia Press in Paris in 1955, edited by 'Count Palmiro Vicarrion', magnanimously offering the tourist public a selection of two hundred limericks, taken and ruthlessly 'improved' from *The Limerick*. A similar '*Bagman's*' volume – a title intended, of course, to twit the present writer – was also issued by the largest foreign-language bookstore in Paris, under the false imprint 'Milan'. The pseudonymous 'Vicarrion' is identified, in recent catalogues of the British bookseller Bernard Stone, as the internationally famous Liverpudlian poet, Mr. Christopher Logue, whose own signed volumes of Angry Young Man (British beatnik) poetry have been compared by *Time* magazine to the *Song of Songs*. I would not go quite so far.

Douglas' collection is nothing so pedestrian. His annotations, which have made the fame of his book, and are in part responsible for the continued popularity of the limerick, are strictly in the

mock-serious style of Dr. Wagstaffe on *Tom Thumb*, Oliver Goldsmith's annotations to *Mother Goose*, and 'To the Critics and
Poets', earlier mentioned, as well as many similar *jeux d'esprit* in
the eighteenth century. There is even a Geographical Index,
similar to that of Cordonnier's *Chef d'Œuvre d'un Inconnu*, tabu-
lating with great seriousness all the sexual and scatological
minutiae of the limerick adventures described. Since the original
publication of *Some Limericks*, privately in Florence in 1928,
there have been many piratical reprints (all listed, in *The Limerick*,
Vol. II, Bibliography, pp. 253–60). One in particular is disguised
under the title, *From Bed to Worse*, printed secretly in Wiesbaden,
in 1945, by 'some members of the Army of Occupation in Germany', as its title-page states; forgetting, however, to mention
Douglas at all. (Copy: Yale.)

A number of slavish imitations, not of Douglas' collection but
of his manner of annotation in mock-serious style, have also been
laboriously assembled and constructed, in manuscript and in
print, most of them infinitely lacking in the wit of Douglas. The
most glaring example is the preface to the 'Vicarrion' collection,
mentioned above, which is almost difficult to credit, in its flat
imitation and grovelling unhumorousness, confusing the mere use
of dirty words and surréalist non-sequiturs with the art of bawdy
humor. An equally bathetic plagiarism of Douglas was issued in
Switzerland in 1944, under the title *A Collection of Limericks*, by
one 'Nosti', a would-be humorist somewhat imperfectly ac-
quainted with the English language, and having the temerity not
only to steal most of Douglas' text and notes, but to attempt to
improve on and paraphase the latter in broken English. The book
is fortunately very rare. (Copy: Collection A. Plesch.)

One very striking lack, in the literature of the limerick, is that of
almost any serious critical writing on the subject, despite the
plethora of mock-pedantic – or do I mean very pedantic? – dis-
cussion of the sexual content of specific bawdy limericks, in the
style of Douglas. The introductions to the usual clean collections,
such as Louis Untermeyer's *Lots of Limericks: Light, Lusty, and
Lasting* (New York, 1961), Bennett Cerf's *Out On a Limerick*
(1960), and Langford Reed's *Complete Limerick Book* (2nd ed.,
London, 1926), which is one of the largest, are mostly twaddle.
On the historical side, they are particularly hopeless, usually
beginning – if not with Lear – with a wholly erroneous genealogy

starting in France in the early eighteenth century, and arriving in Britain via Ireland. As against the century-long development of the limerick form in England from late medieval times, through the sixteenth-century song of the wandering madmen, 'Tom o' Bedlam', exposed in the preceding pages, I do not think the French–Irish genealogical theory will bear scrutiny. As to the general psychology of the limerick, limerick-poets, and limerick-fanciers, the two best early articles are that in the *Encyclopaedia Britannica* (14th ed., 1929), XIV, 130, by Edmund G. V. Knox, later editor of *Punch*; and especially 'The Cult of the Limerick' by C. L. Graves, in the *Cornhill Magazine* (February 1918, vol. 44: No. 260). Valuable information is also brought together, in popular form, in William S. Baring-Gould's *The Lure of the Limerick* (New York, 1967; London, Panther, 1971), which is the first publicly-issued limerick collection courageously to include any bawdy examples without expurgation. The erotic newspaper, *Screw*, the most astonishing product – so far – of the New Freedom in America, also ran a page of bawdy limericks in its No. 22 (New York, 31 July 1969).

The American critic, Clifton Fadiman, writing on the limerick in 'There Was an Old Man of Tobago', in his collection of essays, *Any Number Can Play* (Cleveland, 1957), goes so far as to deny that even Norman Douglas' own notes have any wit about them, and states coldly that 'the book on the whole is a bore that makes its strongest appeal to the phoney Bohemian temperament'. This sounds like treason in the ranks, but the true explanation is probably that Mr. Fadiman likes – and I suspect writes – those god-awful 'clerihews', which are some kind of poetico-prosaic morphodites that only their inventors could love; so perhaps his testimony should be written off as biased. All clerihews being per-fervidly clean, they are all signed and of known authorship, something on the style of the epigraphs one observes in public lavatories: 'I came, I seen, I SAW!!' as found by Dr. Allen Walker Read (*Lexical Evidence from Folk Epigraphy*, Paris, 1935, p. 18) in Timpanogos Cave, northern Utah. This sort of thing is vowed to the swift forgetfulness of a coat of paint, and is folklore only by courtesy. Far different are the anonymous gems of real folk-poetry and epigraphy, scrawled in diamond on the glasses and windows of old English taverns, as recorded in *The Merry-Thought, or The Glass-Window and Bog-House Miscellany* of 1731, in four parts. (Copies: Oxford, and Harding Collection, Chicago; with incomplete copies at Harvard, and British Museum, P.C.) The recently publicly issued 'Graffiti' volumes are all expurgated.

Since World War II, whole clubs have been organized for the perpetuation of bawdy limericks (never of clean ones), and their public annotation – inevitably in the style of Dr. Wagstaffe and Norman Douglas. An amusing phonograph recording has also been issued, under the title *Limerix*, about 1962, by a small American company (Cook), purportedly a tape-recorded transcript of the proceedings of such a limerick club or society, with a harried president trying to run the meeting, and members of both sexes doing the singing and reciting, amid all the usual drinking, fighting, and ego-boost. The tone is, in fact, rather similar to that of the real meetings of such clubs, except for the omitted touch of self-satisfied whimsy in the Annual Norman Douglas Lecture; but the limericks presented – on the recording, at least – are of the mildest possible naughtiness, with all the impact of wet gingersnaps.

The real clubs of this kind have flourished mostly in the American West and Midwest, in particular the American Limerick Society (which met in the home of Dr. MacIntyre in Berkeley, California, during the 1940s), and the Fifth Line Society of Chicago. The last-named, known in full as The Society for the Preservation of the Fifth Line, is the subject of a long explanatory letter or manifesto by one of its members, Mr. Merlin Bowen, in *Evergreen Review* (New York, August 1966), No. 42, pp. 16 and 93, announcing the Society's intention of bringing to public attention in the 'strict iambic pentameter' [?!] of 'action limericks . . . the human side of sadism, the enlarging effects of pederasty, the genetic advantages of lesbianism, and the dietary benefits of fellatio. Most of us, let me say, are ashamed of our callous normality in the past and hope to do better in the future.' If this was not, in fact, the peroration of the Annual Norman Douglas Lecture for 1967, the tone is close enough to serve as an exact sample. Aside from the mock-serious format, all this is of course an outgrowth of the similar college fraternity and army and air-force officers' bawdy-song societies and informal 'beer busts', with their manuscript or mimeographed collections, few of which are ever seen by 'outsiders' or are preserved. One wishes one could somehow convince the college professors, businessmen,

advertising photographers, librarians, and science-fiction en-
thusiasts, who seem to make up most of the membership of these
limerick clubs, that Norman Douglas has now had enough adula-
tion and imitation, and please to lay off.

The only really interesting continuation of Douglas' little jest
so far – and even there the notes are the least successful part of the
imitation – is *That Immoral Garland*, an original manuscript by
the American poet and translator (worth any twenty others today), the late Carlyle Ferren MacIntyre. This manuscript, dated
1942, includes over a hundred of this poet's original bawdy
limericks, of which he was justly proud, in particular the one
beginning 'While Titian was mixing rose-madder' (No. 757 in Vol.
II), which has already entered authentic oral circulation as folklore – something that very few new limericks ever do – and is
probably the best known and most appreciated modern bawdy
limerick.

As can be seen in the 'Titian' prototype, not one of Dr. Mac-
Intyre's limericks begins with the inactive 'There *was* . . .' but
leaps incontinently into the action of the piece from the very first
line on. This attempt to free the limerick from the trammels of its
wasted line – still generally thrown away on the meaningless
affectation of an 'improper' geographical rhyme, as Lear threw
away *both* the first and last lines on the same – is the only real
improvement in the limerick form in over two centuries. Were it
to be continued successfully, this might give the limerick a new
lease on life. As it stands, the only other new element in modern
limericks is purely one of content, imported by an enthusiast
group utterly collegiate in background, which is now also concerning itself with the concoction of bawdy limericks: the science-
fiction fan-club kids, both adolescent and superannuated. Of
their output it can only be said that if the organ-deficiencies and
melancholy accidents of normally bawdy limericks sometimes
make depressing reading, the same *in mathematical symbols*, and
involving complicated quasi-sexual intercourse with mechanical
contraptions and with the blue gleeps and green bleeps of the
planets Mars and Venus, is truly too sad to endure.

Certain rich gifte-booke publishers, such as the late Peter
Beilenson of the over-modestly titled 'Peter Pauper Press', and
most of the theoretically terribly virile 'men's magazines' in
America and Britain, such as *Playboy*, *Penthouse*, and their

mutually incestuous imitations, all of which are expurgated to the
hilt, have also been featuring, since the mid-1950s, volumelets or
a page per issue of mildly bawdy jokes and limericks, more or less
on the Naughty-Naughty style of *The Pink 'Un* in the 1890s, and
all running pretty $tinking $cared, if the truth is to be told. The
best part of these publications is usually the art-work, when this
does not descend to low cartoon-humor, high camp and *kitsch*.
In this line, an extended series of newly-written though not very
off-color limericks appeared in the more than twenty issues of the
bawdy joke-and-cartoon magazine, *Sex to Sexty* (Arlington,
Texas: John Newbern Co.) during the 1960s. Most of these were
written by a San Francisco advertising man, the late John Coulthard (pronounced: Cole-th'rd), who believed, probably correctly,
that he had written the largest number of limericks ever produced
by one person, thus barely getting in ahead of the IBM machine –
'Ten thousand raunchy limericks, and another ten thousand
clean!' his publisher announces proudly, in volume 4 of *Sex to
Sexty* (December 1965), which is cover-titled *Grand Prix Limerix*,
and is devoted entirely to one thousand and one of Coulthard's
'semi-dirty' anonymous originals – meaning dirty, but without
any four-letter words! As an act of dying contrition, Coulthard
then issued privately a large, folding sheet of some of his unexpurgated examples, with erotic cartoon illustrations by himself.
Very few copies of this erotic supplement were printed, nor did it
accompany the *Sex to Sexty* issue, which it makes look very
weak.

Driving hard for the world's record, à new SUPER *Sex to Sexty*
No. 7 was issued in 1969, containing three hundred original off-
color limericks, 'every one illustrated', edited and in part written
by a woman, Peggy 'Goose' Rodebaugh. (The Los Angeles left-
wing collection, *Unexpurgated*, in 1943, had earlier also been co-
edited by a woman.) A 448-page illustrated paperback volume,
reprinting all the limericks that had appeared to date in *Sex to
Sexty* – including John Coulthard's 'semi-dirty' thousand, was
also announced, to include 2,200 examples. This is still, of course,
far from Coulthard's total, or even from that of the present
collection and its Addenda.

The neurotic compulsiveness or gigantism implied in the brag
about writing twenty thousand limericks (in only one lifetime) is
unfortunately no longer the private folly of one limerick poet. In

Baring-Gould's *The Lure of the Limerick*, pp. 109–10, mention is made of a current New York luncheon club, apparently called The Poets Club, 'composed entirely of highly literate business and professional men', whose purpose, aside from a very creditable concern about Shakespeare's reputation as a playwright – every little bit helps – is 'to collect and card-file in their archives every erotic limerick known to English-speaking man'. Perhaps they should begin with John Coulthard's unpublished limericks, which he wrote into large scrapbooks sent to a friend, often in the margins of pages torn from medical works and the like, showing genital diseases and malformations, which the limerick celebrates or reproves. These scrapbooks are now in the possession of his publisher, but nothing seems to have been printed from them. A transcript of the best thousand of these limericks was entrusted to me by Coulthard just before his death, for use in the proposed Addenda volume to the present work. One good limerick out of every ten written is a better average than most poets hit. The best recent unexpurgated limericks I have seen are those of Mr. Jay Thompson, formerly of South Carolina, none of which have as yet been published.

What remains to be said? The future. Have limericks a future? Yes, certainly they have a future, and a livelier present than those damn clerihews! Only in English, of course, though imitations and even translations of both the clean and bawdy forms do exist abroad, oddly enough only in the proto-English languages, Dutch and German. These are definitely imitations and do not date earlier than the present century, being now at the level of a minor newspaper fad. All limericks in French are actually in 'fractured French', by English-speaking poets, and are usually terrible. The worst are those in 'Gorey's' *The Listing Attic*; the best are by George du Maurier, reprinted in Langford Reed's *The Complete Limerick Book*, pp. 68–9, and they are a mark to shoot at for poets who consider this type of ungrammatical language-parody funny. As Prof. Brander Matthews long ago observed, in *A Study of Versification* (1911) p. 145: 'The humble limerick has the distinction of being the only fixed [poetic] form which is actually indigenous to English.' It apparently also intends to stay that way.

It should be clearly understood that rhymed poetry of any kind other than limericks is seldom written today in English, the rhymeless poetry of Walt Whitman's spasmodic school having swept the board. The principal exceptions are the would-be 'popular songs', composed and copyrighted by the tens of thousands (specifically, sixty thousand per year in the U.S.A. alone!) in the delusory hope of monetary gain. These songs no one but their composers ever sings – if them – and the long-suffering public is never even exposed to 99 per cent of them. With this signal exception, the limerick – specifically the bawdy limerick – represents today the principal type and amount of traditionally rhymed poetry being written in the English language, and with any audience. It is also the only newly-composed poetry in English with any chance whatever of oral circulation at the popular level, in traditional folklore fashion, something available to even the most popular of 'popular songs' only for a brief few months or weeks. Meanwhile, dozens of bawdy limericks now anywhere up to a century old are today still being endlessly sung or recited, as old favorites, and their popularity shows no sign of diminishing.

It must of course be admitted that, what with the New Freedom on the one hand making the bawdy limerick's themes and defied repressions somewhat old-hat, and the New Passivity of the media-feedback culture on the other hand making *any* kind of poetry almost too much of an effort for the colorless and unvirile people ('unisex') multiplying like skinned rabbits all around us, the limerick may fall dead and disappear tomorrow. In that case, perhaps this will be the record of its only really popular form in the century of its popularity. For, not to put too fine a point to it, the limerick is not only the only fixed poetic form original to the English language, but the bawdy limerick in particular is today the *only* kind of newly-composed poetry in English, or song, which has the slightest chance whatever of survival.

All in all, one suspects that the limerick of the future will be hopelessly similar to the limerick of the past, and will change merely externally, in the technology and terminology of the horrible castratory accidents over which it all too often gloats. Even so, it would be manifestly unfair to deny to any class, even the educated class, the right to create and circulate whatever folklore and folksong it is capable of, however weakly verbal and uselessly formal the more virile classes might find this folklore to be. The egghead is getting it from all sides: I do not feel his limerick should be taken away from him, or that he should be forced to sing it – just to prove he's one of 'the Boyes', which he isn't –

when, really, he would much prefer to be sitting placidly in the library annotating his limericks with parallel texts from Martial, the *Priapeia*, and the *Greek Anthology*; and never get out and *do* any of the boldly bawdy things mentioned in these limerick fantasies at all.

To avoid the accusation of having cravenly evaded giving any real limericks, in all the dusty library-annotation that has gone before, let me end this essay and open the brawl – as to my errors, 'tone', and so on – by quoting at least one limerick, which is not only authentically erotic, in its mild way, and does not begin with the false and wasted accent of 'There *was* . . .' but has also the remarkable peculiarity of being the favorite limerick of quite a few women, most of whom otherwise loathe limericks (in which they generally figure both as villain and victim), for the same reason that calves hate cookbooks:

> For the tenth time, dull Daphnis, said Chloë,
> You have told me my bosom is snowy;
>   You've made much fine verse on
>   Each part of my person,
> Now *do* something – there's a good boy!

La Clé des Champs
Valbonne (*Alpes-Maritimes*)
FRANCE

SOURCES

This two-volume set is the largest collection of limericks ever published, erotic or otherwise. The seventeen hundred examples gathered here stem, about one-third, from some twenty printed sources dating from 1870 to 1952, most of which duplicate each other to a great extent. The rest are principally from three oral collections, made in Ann Arbor, Michigan (MS. 1938–1941), in Berkeley, California (1942–1947), and in New York (1941–1952). Almost no British materials after 1928 have been available. The chapter-titles are those of *Lapses in Limerick*, the Michigan collection. A chronological list of the sources used follows. Fuller details, and a few minor sources, will be found in the bibliography preceding the notes.

Variant lines, couplets and conclusions are given at the end of the text, with varia in geographical and personal names (in rhyming positions) cited and indexed. Minor variations in phrasing and vocabulary have not seemed worth reporting here. A full Index, of names and rhymes, will be found at the end of the volume, and should make convenient the locating of any desired limerick in spite of the division of the text into chapters. A few folklore parallels are made and explanations given, but humorous and didactic excursi on the style of Norman Douglas' *Some Limericks* (1928) have not been attempted.

Sources are given for each limerick by means of the date. Dates and sources are listed together facing the next page. Where two dates follow a limerick, the second is the actual source of the text; the first is the earliest known variant printing or collecting of it.

These dates have other uses as well, such as turning up all the new limericks in any listed source, or the complete contents of the three known collections of original limericks: *Cythera's Hymnal* (1870), *The Pearl* (1879–1880), and *That Immoral Garland* (MS.

1942A). Chronological changes in the dominant limerick themes over the last eighty years in England and America may also easily be traced, and will provide an unparalleled key to the socio-sexual anxieties of the period.

No improvement has been made upon orally transmitted or printed materials. The limericks are given as found in the sources credited. (Exceptions: punctuation and the spelling of geographical names have been made uniform, expurgations have been spelled out, and the first names of real private persons have been dropped.) The text is eclectic only to the degree of choosing one form – not necessarily the oldest – on which to base all variants. The prejudices, cruelty, and humorless quality of many of the limericks included are deeply regretted. However, no falsification of the material has been made.

THE EDITOR

SOURCES

1870.　*Cythera's Hymnal, or Flakes from the Foreskin.*

1879 to 1880.　*The Pearl* ('Oxford').

1882.　*The Cremorne* ('March 1851').

1910 to 1911.　Dr. SUSRUTA, in *Anthropophyteia.*

1927.　*Immortalia* (Philadelphia).

1927A.　*Anecdota Americana* ('Boston').

1928.　Norman DOUGLAS: *Some Limericks.*

1928A.　'O. U. SCHWEINICKLE': *The Book of 1000 Laughs.*

1928B.　*Poems, Ballads and Parodies* ('Paris, 1923').

1928C.　'Dave E. JONES': *A Collection of Sea Songs.*

1932.　'John FALMOUTH': *Ninety-five Limericks.*

1934.　*Anecdota Americana, Second Series* ('Boston').

1938 to 1941.　*Lapses in Limerick* (MS.)

1939A.　Weston LA BARRE, in *Psychiatry* (May 1939).

1941A.　*Pornographia Literaria* (mimeo).

1942 to 1947.　*Index Limericus* (MS.)

1942A.　*That Immoral Garland* (MS.)

1943A.　*Unexpurgated* (Los Angeles).

1943B.　[Clement WOOD] *The Facts of Life in Limericks.*

1943C.　*An Investigation into . . . Limericks* (mimeo).

1944A to 1948A.　New York (oral collection).

1945C.　*Farmer Gray* (mimeo).

1946B.　[DAVIS] *The International Set.*

1947B.　[HARRISON MS.]

1948.　[MORSE] *The Limerick: A Facet of Our Culture.*

1949.　[DRAKE] *A Book of Anglo-Saxon Verse.*

1950 to 1952.　New York (oral collection).

I STRANGE INTERCOURSE

1

Thus spake I AM THAT I AM:
'For the Virgin I don't give a damn.
　　What pleases Me most
　　Is to bugger the Ghost,
And then be sucked off by the Lamb.'

1928

2

Así dije YO SOY QUE YO SOY:
'Por La Vírgen un carajo no doy.
　　Lo que debe gustar
　　Es Jesús caporar –
Y para hacerlo Yo voy.'

1941

3

Dame Catherine of Ashton-on-Lynches
Got on with her grooms and her wenches:
　　She went down on the gents,
　　And pronged the girls' vents
With a clitoris reaching six inches.

1942A

4

There was a young lady named Astor
Who never let any get past her.
　　She finally got plenty
　　By stopping twenty,
Which certainly ought to last her.

1942

5

Oden the bardling averred
His muse was the bum of a bird,
    And his Lesbian wife
    Would finger his fife
While Fisherwood waited as third.

1942A

6

There was a young fellow named Babbitt
Who could screw nine times like a rabbit,
    But a girl from Johore
    Could do it twice more,
Which was just enough extra to crab it.

1942

7

A young polo-player of Berkeley
Made love to his sweetheart berserkly.
    In the midst of each chukker
    He would break off and fuck her
Horizontally, laterally, and verkeley.

1943

8

There once was a jolly old bloke
Who picked up a girl for a poke.
    He took down her pants,
    Fucked her into a trance,
And then shit in her shoe for a joke.

1941

9

There was a young idler named Blood,
Made a fortune performing at stud,
    With a fifteen-inch peter,
    A double-beat metre,
And a load like the Biblical Flood.

1941

10

Though the invalid Saint of Brac
Lay all of his life on his back,
    His wife got her share,
    And the pilgrims now stare
At the scene, in his shrine, on a plaque.

1943

11

There was an old man of Brienz
The length of whose cock was immense:
    With one swerve he could plug
    A boy's bottom in Zug,
And a kitchen-maid's cunt in Coblenz.

1928

12

There once was a Duchess of Bruges
Whose cunt was incredibly huge.
    Said the King to this dame
    As he thunderously came:
'Mon Dieu! Après moi, le déluge!'

1941

13

There was an old man of Cajon
Who never could get a good bone.
    With the aid of a gland
    It grew simply grand;
Now his wife cannot leave it alone.

1941*

14

There was a young girl of Cape Cod
Who dreamt she'd been buggered by God.
    But it wasn't Jehovah
    That turned the girl over,
'Twas Roger the lodger, the dirty old codger,
The bugger, the bastard, the sod!

1938–1952

15

There once was a lady named Carter,
Fell in love with a virile young Tartar.
  She stripped off his pants,
   At his prick quickly glanced,
And cried: 'For that I'll be a martyr!'

1946A

16

A talented fuckstress, Miss Chisholm,
Was renowned for her fine paroxysm.
  While the man detumesced
   She still spent on with zest,
Her rapture sheer anachronism.

1941

17

There was a young man in the choir
Whose penis rose higher and higher,
  Till it reached such a height
   It was quite out of sight –
But of course you know I'm a liar.

1946A

18

There was a young man from the Coast
Who had an affair with a ghost.
  At the height of orgasm
   Said the pallid phantasm,
'I think I can feel it – almost!'

1942

19

Have you heard of the lady named Cox
Who had a capacious old box?
  When her lover was in place
   She said, 'Please turn your face.
I look like a gal, but I screw like a fox.'

1942

20

A team playing baseball in Dallas
Called the umpire a shit out of malice.
  While this worthy had fits
  The team made eight hits
And a girl in the bleachers named Alice.

                   1946A

21

There was a young girl of Darjeeling
Who could dance with such exquisite feeling
  There was never a sound
  For miles around
Save of fly-buttons hitting the ceiling.

               1943A–1949

22

There was a young woman in Dee
Who stayed with each man she did see.
  When it came to a test
  She wished to be best,
And practice makes perfect, you see.

                   1927

23

There was a family named Doe,
An ideal family to know.
  As father screwed mother,
  She said, 'You're heavier than brother.'
And he said, 'Yes, Sis told me so!'

                   1948

24

A lady, by passion deluded,
Found an African drunk and denuded,
  And – fit as a fiddle,
  And hot for a diddle –
She tied splints to his penis and screwed it.

                   1941

25

There was a strong man of Drumrig
Who one day did seven times frig.
   He buggered three sailors,
   Four Jews and two tailors,
And ended by fucking a pig.

                      1879

26

There was an old man of Duluth
Whose cock was shot off in his youth.
   He fucked with his nose
   And with fingers and toes,
And he came through a hole in his tooth.

                      1941

27

There was an old man of Dundee
Who came home as drunk as could be.
   He wound up the clock
   With the end of his cock,
And buggered his wife with the key.

                  1927–1928

28

A rapturous young fellatrix
One day was at work on five pricks.
   With an unholy cry
   She whipped out her glass eye:
'Tell the boys I can now take on six.'

                  1942–1952

29

There was a young man with a fiddle
Who asked of his girl, 'Do you diddle?'
   She replied, 'Yes, I do
   But prefer to with two –
It's twice as much fun in the middle.'

                  1943A

30

I dined with Lord Hughing Fitz-Bluing
Who said, 'Do you squirm when you're screwing?'
   I replied, 'Simple shagging
   Without any wagging
Is only for screwing canoeing.'

                          1947

31

There was a young fellow named Fletcher,
Was reputed an infamous lecher.
   When he'd take on a whore
   She'd need a rebore,
And they'd carry him out on a stretcher.

                          1943A

32

A young fellow discovered through Freud
That although of a penis devoid,
   He could practice coitus
   By eating a foetus,
And his parents were quite overjoyed.

                          1941

33

There was a young man from Jodhpur
Who found he could easily cure
   His dread diabetes
   By eating a foetus
Served up in a sauce of manure.

                          1945

34

There once was a sailor named Gasted,
A swell guy, as long as he lasted,
   He could jerk himself off
   In a basket, aloft,
Or a breeches-buoy swung from the masthead.

                          1941

35

There was a young girl of Gibraltar
Who was raped as she knelt at the altar.
   It really seems odd
   That a virtuous God
Should answer her prayers and assault her.

1943A

36

A young man with passions quite gingery
Tore a hole in his sister's best lingerie.
   He slapped her behind
   And made up his mind
To add incest to insult and injury.

1941*–1947B

37

A passionate red-headed girl,
When you kissed her, her senses would whirl,
   And her twat would get wet
   And would wiggle and fret,
And her cunt-lips would curl and unfurl.

1941

38

There was a young lady named Gloria
Who was had by Sir Gerald Du Maurier,
   And then by six men,
   Sir Gerald again,
And the band at the Waldorf-Astoria.

1943

39

Thank God for the Duchess of Gloucester,
She obliges all who accost her.
   She welcomes the prick
   Of Tom, Harry or Dick,
Or Baldwin, or even Lord Astor.

1939A

40

The latest reports from Good Hope
State that apes there have pricks thick as rope,
  And fuck high, wide, and free,
  From the top of one tree
To the top of the next – what a scope!

1941

41

A newlywed couple from Goshen
Spent their honeymoon sailing the ocean.
  In twenty-eight days
  They got laid eighty ways –
Imagine such fucking devotion!

1941

42

There was a young fellow named Grimes
Who fucked his girl seventeen times
  In the course of a week –
  And this isn't to speak
Of assorted venereal crimes

1947

43

There was a young lady named Hatch
Who would always come through in a scratch.
  If a guy wouldn't neck her,
  She'd grab up his pecker
And shove the damn thing up her snatch.

1945

44

There was a young lady named Hilda
Who went for a walk with a builder.
  He knew that he could,
  And he should, and he would –
And he did – and he goddam near killed her!

1928A–1941

45

Cum Hilde autem ambulabat
Homo qui ædificabat.
Dixit volebat. Debet et potebat.
Sic ille ducebat. Statim faciebat.
Sed virginem pine necebat.

1941

46

I know of a fortunate Hindu
Who is sought in the towns that he's been to
In the ladies he knows,
Who are thrilled to the toes
By the tricks he can make his foreskin do.

1948A

47

If you're speaking of actions immoral
Then how about giving the laurel
To doughty Queen Esther,
No three men could best her –
One fore, and one aft, and one oral.

1941–1952

48

There was a young miss from Johore
Who'd lie on a mat on the floor;
In a manner uncanny
She'd wobble her fanny,
And drain your nuts dry to the core.

1942

49

There was a young fellow of Kent
Whose prick was so long that it bent,
So to save himself trouble
He put it in double,
And instead of coming he went.

1927–1941

50

There was a young man of Kildare
Who was fucking a girl on the stair.
   The bannister broke,
   But he doubled his stroke
And finished her off in mid-air.

                 1927–1952

51

A young man of Llanfairpwllgwyngyll
While bent over plucking a dingle
   Had the whole Eisteddfod
   Taking turns at his pod
While they sang some impossible jingle.

                 1952

52

There once were two brothers named Luntz
Who buggered each other at once.
   When asked to account
   For this intricate mount,
They said, 'Ass-holes are tighter than cunts.'

                 1941

53

There was a young lady named Mable
Who liked to sprawl out on the table,
   Then cry to her man,
   'Stuff in all you can –
Get your ballocks in, too, if you're able.'

                 1943

54

An impotent Scot named MacDougall
Had to husband his sperm and be frugal.
   He was gathering semen
   To gender a he-man,
By screwing his wife through a bugle.

                 1941

55

There once was a girl named McGoffin
Who was diddled amazingly often.
   She was rogered by scores
   Who'd been turned down by whores,
And was finally screwed in her coffin.

1941

56

A stout Gaelic warrior, McPherson,
Was having a captive, a person
   Who was not averse
   Though she had the curse,
And he'd breeches of bristling furs on.

1942A

57

There was a young Scot in Madrid
Who got fifty-five fucks for a quid.
   When they said, 'Are you faint?'
   He replied, 'No, I ain't,
But I *don't* feel as good as I did.'

1941

58

There was a young fellow of Mayence
Who fucked his own arse, in defiance
   Not only of custom
   And morals, dad-bust him,
But most of the known laws of science.

1949

59

The woman who lives on the moon
Is still cherishing the balloon
   Of an earthling who'd come
   And given her some,
But had dribbled away all too soon.

1942A

60

There is a young faggot named Mose
Who insists that you fuck his long nose.
   And you'll double the joy
   Of this lecherous boy
If you'll tickle his balls with your toes.

1946A

61

There was an Old Man of the Mountain
Who frigged himself into a fountain
   Fifteen times had he spent,
   Still he wasn't content,
He simply got tired of the counting.

1879

62

There was a young lady named Nance
Who learned about fucking in France,
   And when you'd insert it
   She'd squeeze till she hurt it,
And shoved it right back in your pants.

1951

63

A studious professor named Nestor
Bet a whore all his books he could best her.
   But she drained out his balls
   And skipped up the walls,
Beseeching poor Nestor to rest her.

1941A

64

The late Brigham Young was no neuter –
No faggot, no fairy, no fruiter.
   Where ten thousand virgins
   Succumbed to his urgin's
There now stands the great State of Utah.

1941

65

There was a young girl of Newcastle
Whose charms were declared universal.
   While one man in front
   Wired into her cunt,
Another was engaged at her arsehole.

1879

66

There was a young girl from New York
Who plugged up her cunt with a cork.
   A woodpecker or two
   Made the grade, it is true,
But it totally baffled the stork.

Till along came a man who presented
A tool that was strangely indented.
   With a dizzying twirl
   He punctured that girl,
And thus was the cork-screw invented.

1938

68

There was a young girl named O'Clare
Whose body was covered with hair.
   It was really quite fun
   To probe with one's gun,
For her quimmy might be anywhere.

1947

69

There once was a gay young Parisian
Who screwed an appendix incision,
   And the girl of his choice
   Could hardly rejoice
At this horrible lack of precision.

1941

70

While spending the winter at Pau
Lady Pamela forgot to say 'No'.
   So the head-porter made her
   The second-cook laid her;
The waiters were all hanging low.

                    1942A

71

There was a young girl of Penzance
Who boarded a bus in a trance.
   The passengers fucked her,
   Likewise the conductor.
The driver shot off in his pants.

                 1927–1928

72

The Shah of the Empire of Persia
Lay for days in a sexual merger.
   When the nautch asked the Shah,
   'Won't you ever withdraw?'
He replied with a yawn, 'It's inertia.'

                 1938–1941

73

A remarkable race are the Persians,
They have such peculiar diversions.
   They screw the whole day
   In the regular way,
And save up the nights for perversions.

                 1941

74

There was a young girl of Rangoon
Who was blocked by the Man in the Moon.
   'Well, it *has* been great fun,'
   She remarked when he'd done,
'But I'm sorry you came quite so soon.'

                 1928–1941

75

There was a young lady named Ransom
Who was rogered three times in a hansom.
  When she cried out for more
  A voice from the floor
Said, 'My name is Simpson, not Samson.'

1938–1941

76

A maestro directing in Rome
Had a quaint way of driving it home.
  Whoever he climbed
  Had to keep her tail timed
To the beat of his old metronome.

1942A

77

'Last night,' said a lassie named Ruth,
'In a long-distance telephone booth,
  I enjoyed the perfection
  Of an ideal connection –
I was screwed, if you must know the truth.'

1943A

78

Said a Lesbian lady, 'It's sad;
Of all of the girls that I've had,
  None gave me the thrill
  Of real rapture until
I learned how to be a tribade.'

1952

79

There once was a handsome young seaman
Who with ladies was really a demon.
  In peace or in war,
  At sea or on shore,
He could certainly dish out the semen.

1942

80

Said a girl being had in a shanty,
'My dear, you have got it in slanty.'
    He replied, 'I can use
    Any angle I choose.
I ride as I please – I'm Duranty!'

1939A

81

An old couple just at Shrovetide
Were having a piece – when he died.
    The wife for a week
    Sat tight on his peak,
And bounced up and down as she cried.

1942A

82

My wife is an amorous soul
On fire for an African's pole.
    She told a coon chauffeur
    That he was her gopher –
And, say, did he go for her hole!

As he creamed my wife's cunt, the coon said,
'I could fuck this until she was dead!'
    As he plugged up her trough,
    I jerked myself off;
'If *that's* how you feel, go ahead!'

1943B

84

There was a young lady of Spain
Who was fucked by a monk in a drain.
    They did it again,
    And again and again,
And again and again and again.

1943A

85

Mr. Galsworthy rented a suite
In a building devoid of all heat.
   So he fucked for three months,
   Sucked thirty-nine cunts,
Which solved his problem quite neat.

1946A

86

There was a young lady from Sydney
Who could take it right up to her kidney.
   But a man from Quebec
   Shoved it up to her neck.
He had a long one, now didn' he?

1943B–1952

87

There was a young man of Tibet,
And this is the strangest one yet –
   His prick was so long,
   And so pointed and strong,
He could bugger six Greeks *en brochette*.

1941

88

'Tis said that the Emperor Titius
Had a penchant for pleasantries vicious.
   He took two of his nieces
   And fucked them to pieces,
And said it was simply delicious.

1941

89

There was a young man from Toledo
Who was cursed with excessive libido.
   To fuck and to screw,
   And to fornicate too,
Were the three major points of his credo.

1939A

90

A virile young man of Touraine
Had vesicles no one could drain.
  With an unbroken flow
  Thrice the course he would go,
Then roll over and start in again.

1943A

91

'Far dearer to me than my treasure,'
The heiress declared, 'is my leisure.
  For then I can screw
  The whole Harvard crew –
They're slow, but that lengthens the pleasure.'

1941

92

A certain old harpy from Umsk
Who was wholly unable to cumsk
  Would ecstatically shout
  When a samovar spout
Was shoved up her Muscovite rumpsk.

1945

93

A young man with a passion quite vast
Used to talk about making it last,
  Till one day he discovered
  His sister uncovered,
And now he fucks often – and fast.

1948A

94

A galactic patrolman from Venus
Had a hyper-extensible penis.
  Of all forms of life
  Which he'd taken to wife
He preferred a mere woman, from meanness.

1944

95

The sex of the asteroid vermin
Is exceedingly hard to determine.
   The galactic patrol
   Simply fucks any hole
That will possibly let all the sperm in.

1944

96

There was a young fellow from Wark
Who, when he screws, has to bark.
   His wife is a bitch
   With a terrible itch,
So the town never sleeps after dark.

1946A

97

There was a debauched little wench
Whom nothing could ever make blench.
   She admitted men's poles
   At all possible holes,
And she'd bugger, fuck, jerk off, and french.

1943

98

There's an over-sexed lady named Whyte
Who insists on a dozen a night.
   A fellow named Cheddar
   Had the brashness to wed her –
His chance of survival is slight.

1941

99

There was a Hell's Kitchen Y.T.
Who said to two boyfriends, 'Aw, gee,
   I don't think that coitus
   Could possibly hoit us!'
So they did it together, all three.

1943B–1944A

100

A versatile lady of Zaandam
Made appointments completely at random,
   Since if two dates got mixed
   It was easily fixed
By letting them screw her in tandem.

1949

101

While fucking one night, Dr. Zuck
His wife's nipples in his ears stuck.
   Then, his thumb up her bum,
   He could hear himself come,
Thus inventing the Radio Fuck.

Then on further experiment bent,
An improvement he thought he'd invent:
   With his prick as conductor,
   Combed her bush while he fucked her,
And his balls shot off sparks when she spent.

1941

103

Here's to it, and through it, and to it again,
To suck it, and screw it, and screw it again!
   So in with it, out with it,
   Lord work his will with it!
Never a day we don't do it again!

1880–1941*

104

It's only human nature after all
If a fellow puts a girl against the wall
   And puts his inclination
   Into her accommodation
   To increase the population
   Of the rising generation –
Why, it's only human nature after all.

1943–1946A

105   THEY A' DO'T

The grit folk an' the puir do't,
The blyte folk an' the sour do't,
    The black, the white,
    Rude an' polite,
Baith autocrat an' boor do't.

For they a' do't – they a' do't,
The beggars an' the braw do't,
    Folk that ance were,
    An' folk that are –
The folk that come will a' do't.

    The auld folk try't
    The young ane's spy't,
An' straightway kiss an' fa' to't,*
    The blind, the lame,
    The wild, the tame,
In warm climes an' in cauld do't.

The licensed by the law do't,
Forbidden folk an' a' do't,
    An' priest an' nun
    Enjoy the fun,
An' never ance say na' to't.

The goulocks an' the snails do't,
The cushie-doos an' quails do't,
    The dogs, the cats,
    The mice, the rats,
E'en elephants an' whales do't.

The weebit cocks an' hens do't,
The robins an' the wrens do't,
  The grizzly bears,
  The toads an' hares,
The puddocks in the fens do't.

The boars an' kangaroos do't,
The titlins an' cuckoos do't,
  While sparrows sma'
  An' rabbits a'
In countless swarms an' crews do't.

The midges, fleas, an' bees do't,
The mawkes an' mites in cheese do't,
  An' cauld earthworms
  Crawl up in swarms,
An' underneath the trees do't.

The kings an' queens an' a' do't,
The sultan an' Pacha do't,
  An' Spanish dons
  Loup off their thrones
Pu' doon their breeks, an' fa' to't.

For they a' do't – they a' do't,
The grit as weel's the sma' do't,
  Frae crowned king
  To creeping thing,
'Tis just the same – they a' do't!

1832*–1880

II EXCREMENT

115

The Rajah of Afghanistan
Imported a Birmingham can,
  Which he set as a throne
  On a great Buddha stone –
But he crapped out-of-doors like a man.

1942A

116

There was a young lady named Ames
Who would play at the jolliest games.
  She was great fun to lay
  For her rectum would play
Obbligatos, and call you bad names.

1941

117

A young lady who lived in Astoria
Took a fancy to Fletcher's Castoria.
  She partook of this drink
  With her ass in the sink –
Now I ask you: ain't that foresight for ya?

1948A

118

When a woman in strapless attire
Found her breasts working higher and higher,
  A guest, with great feeling,
  Exclaimed, 'How appealing!
Do you mind if I piss in the fire?'

1945

119

Sir Reginald Barrington Bart.
Went to the masked ball as a fart.
    He had painted his face
    Like a more private place,
And his voice made the dowagers start.

1942A

120

There was a young fellow named Bart
Who strained every shit through a fart.
    Each tip-tapered turd
    Was the very last word
In this deft and most intricate art.

1941

121

There was a young man of Bhogat,
The cheeks of whose ass were so fat
    That they had to be parted
    Whenever he farted,
And propped wide apart when he shat.

1879–1941

122

A cabman who drove in Biarritz
Once frightened a fare into fits.
    When reprov'd for a fart,
    He said, 'God bless my heart,
When I break wind I usually shits.'

1879

123

There was a young fellow named Brewster
Who said to his wife as he goosed her,
    'It used to be grand
    But just look at my hand;
You ain't wiping as clean as you used to.'

1942

124

A nasty young joker named Bruce
Used to greet all his friends with a goose,
   Till it came to a stop
   In a handful of flop
From some bowels that were terribly loose.

1948A

125

There was a fat lady of Bryde
Whose shoelaces once came untied.
   She didn't dare stoop
   For fear she would poop,
And she cried and she cried and she cried.

1927–1941

126

There was a young man of Bulgaria
Who once went to piss down an area.
   Said Mary to cook,
   'Oh, do come and look,
Did you ever see anything hairier?'

1880

127

There was a young friar of Byhill
Who went up to shit on a high hill.
   When the abbot asked, 'Was it
   A goodly deposit?'
He said, '*Vox et praeterea nihil.*'

1941

128

There was an old Bey of Calcutta
Who greased up his asshole with butter.
   Instead of the roar
   Which came there before,
Came a soft, oleaginous mutter.

1946B

129

There once was a horse from Cape Verdes
Who produced most unusual turds,
   By the simplest means
   He'd eat corn and beans
And make succotash for the birds.

                             1947B

130

A tourist who stopped at Capri
Was had by an old maid for tea.
   When she wiggled he said,
   As he patted her head,
'Ah, you're changing the "t" to a "p"!'

                             1942A

131

There was a young man named Cattell
Who knew psychophysics so well,
   That each time he shit
   He'd stop, measure it –
Its length, and its breadth, and its smell.

                             1939A

132

An efficient young fellow named Cave
Said, 'Think of the time that I save
   By avoiding vacations
   And sexy relations,
And taking a crap while I shave.'

                             1945

133

There was a young fellow named Charted
Who rubbed soap on his bung when it smarted,
   And to his surprise
   He received a grand prize,
For the bubbles he blew when he farted.

                             1941

134

A nasty old bugger of Cheltenham
Once shit in his bags as he knelt in 'em.
    So he sold 'em at Ware
    To a gentleman there
Who didn't much like what he smelt in 'em.

1870

135

There was a young fellow of Chiselhurst
Who never could piss till he'd whistle first.
    One evening in June
    He lost track of the tune –
Dum-da-de-dee . . . and his bladder burst!

1941

136

There was a young fellow named Chivy
Who, whenever he went to the privy,
    First solaced his mind,
    And then wiped his behind,
With some well-chosen pages of Livy.

1946B

137

Said the Duke to the Duchess of Chypre,
'Now, can-paper's grand for a wiper,
    But I don't give a damn for
    This new-fangled camphor-
and-menthol impregnated paper.'

Said the Duchess, 'Well yes, I daresay
Plain bum-wad's all right in its way,
    But there's nothing so grand
    As some leaves, or your hand,
When you're out in the woods for a day.'

1941

139

A young bio-chemist named Dan
Always followed his nose to the can.
   He judged people best
   By the urinal test,
As to race and to sex and to clan.

                 1941*

140

There was a faith-healer of Deal
Who said, 'Although pain isn't real,
   When, frightened by chance,
   I unload in my pants,
I dislike what I fancy I feel.'

                 1941

141

There was an old person of Delhi
Awoke with a pain in his belly,
   And to cure it, 'tis said,
   He shit in his bed,
And the sheets were uncommonly smelly.

                 1870

142

There was a young lady of Dexter
Whose husband exceedingly vexed her,
   For whenever they'd start
   He'd unfailingly fart
With a blast that damn nearly unsexed her.

                 1941

143

There was a young lady of Dorset
Who went to an Underground closet.
   She screwed up her ass
   But passed only some gas,
And *that* wasn't tuppence-worth, was it?

                 1941

144

There was a young woman named Dottie
Who said as she sat on her potty,
   'It isn't polite
   To do this in sight,
But then, who am I to be snotty?'

1946A

145

My neighbors, the dirty Miss Drews,
Stand on their door-step and muse,
   And tie up their tresses
   While the dogs make their messes,
And I am wiping my shoes.

1936*

146

There was a young fellow of Ealing,
Devoid of all delicate feeling.
   When he read on the door:
   'Don't shit on the floor'
He jumped up and shat on the ceiling.

1941

147

The Marquesa de Excusador
Used to pee on the drawing-room floor,
   For the can was so cold
   And when one grows old
To be much alone is a bore.

1942A

148

While watching some tragical farces,
The audience had a catharsis.
   Instead of real tears
   They wept with their rears,
Which proves that catharsis my arse is.

1942–1951

149

There was a young lady of Fismes
Who amazingly voided four streams.
    A friend poked around
    And a fly-button found
Wedged tightly in one of her seams.

1941

150

There was a young lady from France
Supposed to play at a dance,
    She ate a banana
    And played the piano
And music came out of her pants.

1946A

151

There was a young lady of Ghat
Who never could sit but she shat.
    Oh, the seat of her drawers
    Was a chamber of horrors,
And they felt even fouler than that!

1941

152

There once was a fellow named Glantz
Who on entering a toilet in France,
    Was in such a heat
    To paper the seat,
He shit right into his pants.

1941*

153

Alas for a preacher named Hoke,
Whose shit was all stuck in his poke.
    He farted a blast
    That left hearers aghast,
But nothing emerged but some smoke.

1941

154

A professor who taught at Holyoke
Had a bung like a red artichoke.
   She was greatly annoyed
   That each ripe haemorrhoid
Always quivered whenever she spoke.

                         1942A

155

There once was a builder named Howell
Who had a remarkable bowel.
   He built him a building
   Of brickwork and gilding
Using – what do you think – on his trowel.

                         1947B

156

That illustrious author, Dean Howells,
Had a terrible time with his bowels.
   His wife, so they say,
   Cleaned them out every day
With special elongated trowels.

                         1932

157

Here's to the State of Iowa
Whose soil is soft and rich.
   We need no turd
   From your beautiful bird,*
You red headed son of a bitch.

                         1928A

158

There was a young man from Kilbryde
Who fell in a shit house and died.
   His heart-broken brother
   Fell into another,
And now they're interred side by side

                     1925*–1941

159

There was a young girl of La Plata
Who was widely renowned as a farter.
  Her deafening reports
  At the Argentine sports
Made her much in demand as a starter.

1941

160

Q. Flaccus in his third *liber*:
'The Romans have no wood-pulp fiber.
  A crapulent quorum
  Will squat in the Forum
And heave dirty stones in the Tiber.'

1942A

161

There was a young man of Loch Leven
Who went for a walk about seven.
  He fell into a pit
  That was brimful of shit,
And now the poor bugger's in heaven.

1928

162

An old G.I. custom long-rooted
Is to entering fledglings well-suited.
  In every latrine
  A bright sign is seen:
'Stand close, the next guy may be barefooted.'

1943

163

There was a young Georgian named Lynd
Who'd never in all his life sinned,
  For whenever he'd start
  He'd be jarred by a fart,
And his semen was gone with the wind.

1941

164

There was a young man named McBride
Who could fart whenever he tried.
    In a contest he blew
    Two thousand and two,
And then shit and was disqualified.

1945c

165

There was a young man named McFee
Who was stung in the balls by a bee.
    He made oodles of money
    By oozing pure honey
Every time he attempted to pee.

1943A

166

There was a young girl of Machias
Whose bloomers were cut on the bias,
    With an opening behind
    To let out the wind,
And to let the boys in once or twias.

1938

167

There was a young fellow named Malcolm
Who dusted his ass-hole with talcum.
    He'd always use it
    Everytime that he shit,
And found the sensation right welcome.

1943

168

There was an old man of Madrid
Who went to an auction to bid.
    In the first lot they sold
    Was an ancient commode –
And, my god, when they lifted the lid!

1941

169

There was a young Royal Marine
Who tried to fart 'God Save the Queen.'
   When he reached the soprano
   Out came the guano,
And his breeches weren't fit to be seen.

                                  1879–1928

170

There is a professor named Martin
From whom I'm about to be partin',
   And on my way out
   He may hear me shout,
'It's your face I'd sure like to fart in.'

                                  1943

171

A movement once rose 'mongst the masses
To travel about with bare asses.
   At true lovers' parting
   The best form was farting,
With buttocks immersed in molasses.

                                  1941*

172

A gay young blade from Milano
Was Count Galeazzo Ciano.
   Safe from the wars,
   He found that his drawers
Contained rich deposits of guano.

                                  1946B

173

There once was a lady named Muir
Whose mind was so frightfully pure
   That she fainted away
   At a friend's house one day
When she saw some canary manure.

                                  1939A

174

There was a young lady of Newcastle
Who wrapped up a turd in a parcel,
   And sent it to a relation
   With this invitation –
'It has just come out hot from my arsehole.'

                           1870

175

There was an old scholar named Nick
Who wrote Latin and Greek with his prick.
   He peed a paean
   In the snow by a john
In script more than three inches thick.

                           1941

176

An eminent preacher named Nixon
Used to fart as he said benediction.
   The shy flock would smile
   As they trooped down the aisle:
'The arse on our parson needs fixin'.'

                           1942A

177

There was a young girl in Ohio
Whose baptismal name was Maria.
   She would put on airs
   And pee on the stairs,
If she thought that no one was nigh 'er.

                           1927

178

There was a young lady of Pinner,
Who dreamt that her lover was in her.
   This excited her heart,
   So she let a great fart,
And shit out her yesterday's dinner.

                           1870

179

There was an old man who could piss
Through a ring – and, what's more, never miss.
    People came by the score,
    And bellowed, 'Encore!
Won't you do it again, Sir? Bis! Bis!'

1928

180

There was a young lady of Purdbright
Who never could quite get her turd right.
    She'd go to the closet
    And leave a deposit
Like a mouse or a bat or a bird might.

1941

181

There was an old fellow of Pittwood
Who never was able to shit good.
    He'd leave small deposits
    On shelves and in closets,
As a very small pup or a kit would.

1949

182

There was a young man of Rangoon
Whose farts could be heard to the moon.
    When least you'd expect 'em,
    They'd burst from his rectum
With the force of a raging typhoon.

1941

183

There was a young man of Rangoon
Who farted and filled a balloon.
    The balloon went so high
    That it stuck in the sky,
And stank out the Man in the Moon.

1879

184

There was an old fellow from Roop
Who'd lost all control of his poop.
    One evening at supper
    His wife said, 'Now, Tupper,
Stop making that noise with your soup!'
                              1927–1941

185

The intestines of Dante Rossetti
Were exceedingly fragile and petty.
    All he could eat
    Was finely chopped meat,
And all he could shit was spaghetti.

                                    1932

186

There was a young man from St. Paul
Who had really no scruples at all –
    He would fart when he'd talk,
    And shit when he'd walk,
And at night throw it over the wall.
                              1943–1952

187

There was an old soldier named Schmitt
Took a trip to the can for to shit.
    To his epic despair
    No paper was there,
So he simply continued to sit.

                              1943–1951

188

Tom, Tom, the piper's son,
Let loose a fart, and away he run.
    But Tom fell in
    An old shit bin
And ever since then Tom stinks like sin!
                                  1941*

189   THE FARTER FROM SPARTA

There was a young fellow from Sparta,
A really magnificent farter,
  On the strength of one bean
   He'd fart God Save the Queen,
And Beethoven's Moonlight Sonata.

He could vary, with proper persuasion,
His fart to suit any occasion.
  He could fart like a flute,
   Like a lark, like a lute,
This highly fartistic Caucasian.

This sparkling young farter from Sparta,
His fart for no money would barter.
  He could roar from his rear
   Any scene from Shakespeare,
Or Gilbert and Sullivan's Mikado.

He'd fart a gavotte for a starter,
And fizzle a fine serenata.
  He could play on his anus
   The Coriolanus:
Oof, boom, er-tum, tootle, yum tah-dah!

He was great in the Christmas Cantata,
He could double-stop fart the Toccata,
  He'd boom from his ass
   Bach's B-Minor Mass,
And in counterpoint, La Traviata.

Spurred on by a very high wager
With an envious German named Bager,
   He proceeded to fart
   The complete oboe part
Of a Haydn Octet in B-major.

His repertoire ranged from classics to jazz,
He achieved new effects with bubbles of gas.
   With a good dose of salts
   He could whistle a waltz
Or swing it in razzamatazz.

His basso profundo with timbre so rare
He rendered quite often, with power to spare.
   But his great work of art,
   His fortissimo fart,
He saved for the Marche Militaire.

One day he was dared to perform
The William Tell Overture Storm,
   But naught could dishearten
   Our spirited Spartan,
For his fart was in wonderful form.

It went off in capital style,
And he farted it through with a smile,
   Then, feeling quite jolly,
   He tried the finale,
Blowing double-stopped farts all the while.

The selection was tough, I admit,
But it did not dismay him one bit,
   Then, with ass thrown aloft
   He suddenly coughed . . .
And collapsed in a shower of shit.

His bunghole was blown back to Sparta,
Where they buried the rest of our farter,
   With a gravestone of turds
   Inscribed with the words:
'To the Fine Art of Farting, A Martyr.'
                     1938–1948A

201

The damned Jap sons-a-bitches,
We made them wet their britches.
   We grabbed our gun,
   And made 'em run,
The goddamned sons-a-bitches.

                     1943*

202

There was a young man from Split
Who was thrilled with the thought of a shit.
   He was simply elated,
   Till he grew constipated,
But that took all the pleasure from it.

                     1943

203

A keen-scented dean of Tacoma
Was awarded a special diploma
   For his telling apart
   Of a masculine fart
From a similar female aroma.

                     1947

204

I sat by the Duchess at tea,
And she asked, 'Do you fart when you pee?'
  I said with some wit,
  'Do you belch when you shit?'
And felt it was one up for me.

1928–1941

205

When asked by the Duchess at tea
If an eggplant I ever did see,
  I said 'Yes,' rather bored;
  She said, 'Sir, you've explored
Up a hen's ass much further than me.'

1946B

206

There was a young man from Ti' Juana
Who declared as he wallowed in guano,
  'It may seem imbecilic
  To be *so* coprophilic –
I indulge in it just 'cause I wanna.'

1948A

207

There was a young fellow named Twyss
Whose orgasms forced him to piss,
  And most girls objected
  To having injected
A flood of his piss 'midst their bliss.

But one girl – a smart little floozie –
Saw reason for being less choosey.
  Said this sensible miss,
  'Well, anyway, Chris,
Your piss certn'y cleans out my coosie.'

1941

209

'It's true,' confessed Jane, Lady Torres,
'That often I beg lifts in lorries.
   When the men stop to piss
   I see things that I miss
When I travel alone in my Morris.'

                            1947A

210

There once was a sailor from Wales,
An expert at pissing in gales.
   He could piss in a jar
   From the top-gallant spar
Without even wetting the sails.

                            1941

211

There was an old lady from Wheeling
Who had a peculiar feeling,
   She laid on her back
   And opened her crack
And pissed all over the ceiling.

                       1870–1925*

212

There was an old lady of Ypres
Who got shot in the ass by some snipers,
   And when she blew air
   Through the holes that were there,
She astonished the Cameron Pipers.

                            1941

III   ZOOPHILY

213

There was a young man of Adair
Who thought he would diddle a mare.
   He climbed up a ladder
   And jolly well had her,
With his backside a-wave in the air.

1941

214

There was a young man of Australia
Who went on a wild bacchanalia.
   He buggered a frog,
   Two mice and a dog,
And a bishop in fullest regalia.

1941

215

There once was a sacred baboon
That lived by the river Rangoon,
   And all of the women
   That came to go swimmin'
He'd bang by the light of the moon.

1941

216

There was a young man from Bangore
Who was tired and said to his whore,
   'If you'll only roll over
   I'll get my dog Rover,
And you can have six inches more.'

1939A

217

There once was a man of Belfast
Whose balls out of iron were cast.
  He'd managed somehow
  To bugger a sow,
Thus you get pig-iron, at last.

1947ʙ

218

There was a young man of Bengal
Who went to a fancy dress ball.
  Just for a stunt
  He dressed up as a cunt
And was fucked by a dog in the hall.

1928–1932

219

A habit obscene and bizarre
Has taken a-hold of papa:
  He brings home young camels
  And other odd mammals,
And gives them a go at mama.

1946*–1947

220

The Communist Party's Earl Browder
Was fucking a girl in a howda.
  The elephant's trunk
  Somehow got in her cunt
Which, they felt, made it terribly crowded.

1948ᴀ

221

There was a young gaucho named Bruno
Who said, 'Screwing is one thing I *do* know.
  A woman is fine,
  And a sheep is divine,
But a llama is Numero Uno.'

1942ᴀ–1944ᴀ

222

Said an old taxidermist in Burrell,
As he skilfully mounted a squirrel,
   'This excess of tail is
   Obstructive to phallus;
One's much better off with a girl.'

1942A

223

There was an old man of the Cape
Who buggered a Barbary ape.
   The ape said, 'You fool!
   You've got a square tool;
You've buggered my arse out of shape.'

1879–1928

224

A fisherman off of Cape Cod
Said, 'I'll bugger that tuna, by God!'
   But the high-minded fish
   Resented his wish,
And nimbly swam off with his rod.

1942A

225

There once was a man of Cape Nod
Who attempted to bugger a cod,
   When up came some scallops
   And nibbled his bollops,
And now he's a eunuch, by God.

1930*–1951

226

Minnehaha was washing her clothes,
Unexpectant of sorrows or woes.
   A snake, a side-winder,
   Crawled in her behinder,
Wiggled 'round and came out of her nose.

1946A

227

A sailor indulged in coitus
With a cow of the genus of Cetus.
   Piscatologists thundered,
   Biologists wondered,
At the anchor tattooed on the foetus.

1942A

228

A man who was richer than Croesus
Enjoyed being sucked off by feices,
   Till a vicious old hound
   Thought his stake was ground round,
And chewed it completely to pieces.

1942

229

There once was a fairy named Cyril
Who was had in a wood by a squirrel,
   And he liked it so good
   That he stayed in the wood
Just as long as the squirrel was virile.

1941

230

There once was a clergyman's daughter
Who detested the pony he bought her
   Till she found that its dong
   Was as hard and as long
As the prayers her father had taught her.

She married a fellow named Tony
Who soon found her fucking the pony.
   Said he, 'What's it got,
   My dear, that I've not?'
Sighed she, 'Just a yard-long bologna.'

1941

232

That Harvard don down at El Djim –
Oh, wasn't it nasty of him,
   With the whole hareem randy,
   The sheik himself handy,
To muss up a young camel's quim?

                    1942A

233

The eminent Mrs. DeVue
Was born in a cage at the zoo,
   And the curious rape
   Which made her an ape
Is highly fantastic, if true.

                    1945A

234

There was a young girl of Dundee
Who was raped by an ape in a tree.
   The result was most horrid –
   All ass and no forehead,
Three balls and a purple goatee.

                    1938

235

Pine insulensis inevit
Rectum simioli quem scivit
   Proles infrontata
   Horrida glandata
Et semper violare cupivit.

                    1941

236

The prior of Dunstan St. Just,
Consumed with erotical lust,
   Raped the bishop's prize fowls,
   Buggered four startled owls
And a little green lizard, that bust.

                    1948A

237

There was a young girl of Eau Claire
Who once was attacked by a bear.
　　While chased in a field
　　She tripped and revealed
Some meat to the bear that was rare.

1944A

238

There was a young man of Eau Claire
Who had an affair with a bear,
　　But the surly old brute
　　With a snap of her snoot
Left him only one ball and some hair.

1927–1947B

239

When Theocritus guarded his flock
He piped in the shade of a rock.
　　It is said that his Muse
　　Was one of the ewes
With a bum like a pink hollyhock.

1942A

240

There was a young lady named Florence
Who for fucking professed an abhorrence,
　　But they found her in bed
　　With her cunt flaming red,
And her poodle-dog spending in torrents.

1941

241

There once was a fellow named Fogg
Who attempted to bugger a hog.
　　While engaged in his frolics
　　The hog ate his bollix,
And now he's a eunuch, by God.

1930*–1946A

242

One morning Mahatma Gandhi
Had a hard-on, and it was a dandy.
  So he said to his aide,
  'Please bring me a maid,
Or a goat, or whatever is handy.'

1941

243

There once was a man of Geneva
Who buggered a black bitch retriever.
  The result was a sow,
  Two horses, a cow,
Three lambs and a London coal-heaver.

1930*–1952

244

There was a young peasant named Gorse
Who fell madly in love with his horse.
  Said his wife, 'You rapscallion,
  That horse is a stallion –
This constitutes grounds for divorce.'

1941–1951

245

There was an old man from near here,
Got awfully drunk upon beer.
  He fell in a ditch
  And a son of a bitch
Of a bull dog fucked him in the ear.

1928ʙ

246

The Mahatma on Mt. Himavat
Opined as he diddled a cat:
  'She's a far better piece
  Than the Viceroy's niece,
Who has also more fur on her prat.'

1942ᴀ

247

A fox-hound retired from the hunt
For he found that his lobes had grown blunt
    To the scent of the fox,
    But he still would sniff rocks
For the mystical fragrance of cunt.

1942A

248

There was a young man with the itch
Who, because he was not at all rich,
    Had to harbor his tail
    In any female –
A duck or a sow or a bitch.

1941

249

There was a young fellow named Jim
Whose wife kept a worm in her quim.
    It was silly and smelly,
    And tickled her belly,
And what the hell was it to *him*?

1944A

250

A spinster in Kalamazoo
Once strolled after dark by the zoo.
    She was seized by the nape,
    And raped by an ape,
And she murmured, 'A wonderful screw.'

And she added, 'You're rough, yes, and hairy,
But I hope – yes I do – that I marry
    A man with a prick
    Half as stiff and as thick
As the kind that you zoo-keepers carry.'

1941

252

All the lady-apes ran from King Kong
For his dong was unspeakably long.
    But a friendly giraffe
    Quaffed his yard and a half,
And ecstatically burst into song.

                                        1941

253

Said a lovely young lady named Lake,
Pervertedly fond of a snake,
    'If my good friend, the boa,
    Shoots spermatozoa,
What offspring we'll leave in our wake!'

Another young lady would make
Advances to snake after snake.
    Though men she had met
    Got her diaphragm wet,
She wanted her glottis to shake.

                                    1928–1941

255

In a meadow a man named Llewellyn
Had a dream he was bundling with Helen.
    When he woke he discovered
    A bull had him covered
With ballocks as big as a melon.

                                        1942A

256

There was an old Scot named McTavish
Who attempted an anthropoid ravish.
    The object of rape
    Was the wrong sex of ape,
And the anthropoid ravished McTavish.

                                        1948A

257

There was a young man, a Maltese,
Who could even screw horses with ease.
  He'd flout natural laws
  In this manner because
Of his dong, which hung down to his knees.

1943A

258

Thus spake an old Chinese mandarin,
'There's a subject I'd like to use candor in:
  The geese of Pekin
  Are so steepèd in sin
They'd as soon let a man as a gander in.'

1941

259

Here's to old King Montezuma,
For fun he would bugger a puma.
  The puma in play
  Clawed both balls away –
How's that for animal humor?

1948–1950

260

There was a young lady of Mott
Who inserted a fly up her twat
  And pretended the buzz
  Was not what it was
But something she knew it was not.

1943–1949

261

There was a young lady named Myrtle
Who had an affair with a turtle.
  She had crabs, so they say,
  In a year and a day,
Which proves that the turtle was fertile.

1927–1941

262

There was a young man from Nantucket
Took a pig in a thicket to fuck it.
   Said the pig, 'Oh, I'm queer,
   Get away from my rear . . .
Come around to the front and I'll suck it.'

1941

263

There once was a laddie of Neep
Who demanded everything cheap.
   When he wanted to screw
   There was nothing to do
But take out his passion on sheep.

1951

264

There was a young man from New Haven
Who had an affair with a raven.
   He said with a grin
   As he wiped off his chin,
'Nevermore!'

1943c

265

There was a young man of Newminster Court
Bugger'd a pig, but his prick was too short.
   Said the hog, 'It's not nice,
   But pray take my advice:
Make tracks, or by the police you'll be caught.'

1879

266

An elderly pervert in Nice
Who was long past desire for a piece
   Would jack-off his hogs,
   His cows and his dogs,
But his parrot called in the police.

1942a

267

There was a young man named O'Rourke,
Heard babies were brought by the stork,
   So he went to the zoo
   And attempted to screw
One old bird – end-result: didn't work.

1951

268

The notorious Duchess of Peels
Saw a fisherman fishing for eels.
   Said she, 'Would you mind? –
   Shove one up my behind.
I am anxious to know how it feels.'

1944A

269

There was a young man in Peru
Who had nothing whatever to do,
   So he flew to the garret
   And buggered the parrot,
And sent the result to the zoo.

1879–1941

270

A gruff anthropoid of Piltdown
Had a strange way of going to town:
   With maniacal howls
   He would bugger young owls,
And polish his balls on their down.

1942

271

There was a young Nubian prince
Whose cock would make elephants wince.
   Once, while socking the sperm
   To a large pachyderm,
He slipped, and he's not been seen since

1943A

272

There was an old hostler named Rains,
Possessed of more ballocks than brains.
    He stood on a stool
    To bugger a mule,
And got kicked in the balls for his pains.

1941

273

There once was a girl named Miss Randall
Who kept a young bear cub to dandle.
    She said, 'In a pinch
    This bear cub's six-inch
Is almost as good as a candle.'

1944

274

There was a young lady of Rhodes
Who sinned in unusual modes.
    At the height of her fame
    She abruptly became
The mother of four dozen toads.

1943A

275

A nigger in fair St. Domingo
Being blasé and worn said, 'By Jingo,
    Blast all women and boys,
    I'll try some new joys.'
So he went out and fucked a Flamingo.

1880

276

There was a young man of St. John's
Who wanted to bugger the swans.
    But the loyal hall-porter
    Said, 'Pray take my daughter!
Them birds are reserved for the dons.'

1928–1941

277

There was a young man of St. Paul
Whose prick was exceedingly small.
   He could bugger a bug
   At the edge of a rug,
And the bug hardly felt it at all.

                 1927–1941

278

A hermit who lived on St. Roque
Had a lily perfected to poke.
   He diddled the donkeys
   And meddled with monkeys,
And would have done worse, but it broke.

                 1942A

279

There was an old man of Santander
Who attempted to bugger a gander.
   But that virtuous bird
   Plugged its ass with a turd,
And refused to such low tastes to pander.

There was a young man from Toulouse
Who thought he would diddle a goose.
   He hunted and bunted
   To get the thing cunted,
But decided it wasn't no use.

                 1879–1941

281

There was an old person of Sark
Who buggered a pig in the dark.
   The swine, in surprise,
   Murmured, 'God blast your eyes,
Do you take me for Boulton or Park?'

                 1879

282

There once was a sergeant named Schmitt
Who wanted a crime to commit.
  He thought raping women
  Was a little too common,
So he buggered an aged tomtit.

1944

283

There was a young lady named Schneider
Who often kept trysts with a spider.
  She found a strange bliss
  In the hiss of her piss,
As it strained through the cobwebs inside her.

1941

284

When Brother John wanted a screw
He would stuff a fat cat in a shoe,
  Pull up his cassock
  And kneel on a hassock,
Trying his damnedest to mew.

1942A

285

There was a young man of Seattle
Who bested a bull in a battle.
  With fire and gumption
  He assumed the bull's function,
And deflowered a whole herd of cattle.

1945

286

There was a young girl from Seattle
Whose hobby was sucking off cattle.
  But a bull from the South
  Left a wad in her mouth
That made both her ovaries rattle.

1941*–1946B

287

If Gracie Allen were the last of her sex,
And I were the last of mine,
   I'd ease my tool
   By fucking a mule
Or even a porcupine.

               1939A

288

A rooster residing in Spain
Used to diddle his hens in the rain.
   'I give them a bloody
   Good time when it's muddy:
Which keeps them from getting too vain.'

               1942A

289

There once was a Dutchman named Spiegle
Who slept with an elegant beagle.
   As they crawled into bed
   He wistfully said,
'It'll be much better if you wiggle.'

               1942

290

Said the famous composer, R. Strauss
When asked why he buggered a mouse:
   'Though its cunt is quite tiny
   On occasion its heiny
Will stretch quite as big as a house.'

               1948A

291

There was a young lady named Sutton
Who said, as she carved up the mutton,
   'My father preferred
   The last sheep in the herd –
This is one of his children I'm cuttin'.'

               1948A

292

When Jupiter hid in a swan
And laid Leda low on the lawn,
   Pled she, 'Stick your neck in,
   But please do not peck in
My box, for the lining is gone.'

                  1942A

293

There was a young lady from Teal
Who was raped in the lake by an eel.
   One morning at dawn
   She gave birth to a prawn,
Two crabs, and a small baby seal.

            1939A–1941

294

As the rabbi was cutting the throat
Of the annual tribal scape-goat,
   Said the beast, 'I will cite you
   As a sodomite! You
Forget what we did on the boat.'

                  1942A

295

A novelist from Tortilla Flats
Repeatedly buggered stray cats.
   The alley-fence howls
   As he stirred up their bowels
Enormously pleased the town rats.

                  1940*

296

A broken-down harlot named Tupps
Was heard to confess in her cups:
   'The height of my folly
   Was fucking a collie –
But I got a nice price for the pups.'

                  1941

297

A vice both obscene and unsavory
Holds the Mayor of Southampton in slavery.
    With bloodcurdling howls
    He deflowers young owls
Which he keeps in an underground aviary.

1939*

298

A sheep-herder out in Van Buren
Lost half of his flock with the murrain.
    Quoth the state veterinary,
    'You ought not to carry
Them live spirochetes of your'n!'

1942A

299

There was a young artist named Victor
Who purchased a boa constrictor.
    He intended to sketch her,
    But decided (the lecher!)
To fuck her instead of depict her.

1943A

300

A promiscuous person named Willie
Had a dong that was simply a dilly.
    He would take on all mammals
    And was partial to camels,
But they never could tolerate Willie.

1942–1952

301

There was a young lady of Wohl's Hill
Who sat herself down on a mole's hill.
    The resident mole
    Stuck his head up her hole –
The lady's all right, but the mole's ill.

1951

302

There was a young man in Woods Hole
Who had an affair with a mole.
   Though a bit of a nancy
   He *did* like to fancy
Himself in a dominant role.

1951

303

You've heard of the Duchess of York,
She's twice been blessed by the stork.
   The Duke will fuck
   Naught else but a duck,
While the Duchess she frequents the park.

1939A

304

A keeper in Hamburg's great zoo
Tried to have a young girl kangaroo.
   But she zipped up her pouch,
   And the rascal said, 'Ouch!
You've got a half peter in you.'

1942A

IV GOURMANDS

305

There was a young sapphic named Anna
Who stuffed her friend's cunt with banana,
   Which she sucked bit by bit
   From her partner's warm slit,
In the most approved lesbian manner.

1934–1941

306

There was a young girl of Antietam
Who liked horse turds so well she could eat 'em.
   She'd lie on their rumps
   And swallow the lumps
As fast as the beasts could excrete 'em.

1947B

307

There was a young man had the art
Of making a capital tart
   With a handful of shit,
   Some snot and a spit,
And he'd flavor the whole with a fart.

1879

308

There was an old man of Balbriggan,
Who cunt juice was frequently swigging,
   But even to this
   He preferred tom-cat's piss,
Which he kept a pox'd nigger to frig in.

1879

309

There once was a midget named Carr
Who couldn't reach up to the bar,
　　So in every saloon
　　He climbed a spittoon,
And guzzled his liquor from thar.

1939A

310

There was a young man from the coast
Who ate melted shit on his toast.
　　When the toast saw the shit
　　It collapsed in a fit,
For the shit was its grandfather's ghost.

1934

311

There was an old man of Corfu
Who fed upon cunt-juice and spew.
　　When he couldn't get that,
　　He ate what he shat –
And bloody good shit he shat, too.

On clinkers his choice often fell,
Or clabbered piss brought to a jell.
　　When these palled to his taste
　　He tried snot and turd-paste,
And found them delicious as well.

He ate them, and sighed, and said, 'What
Uncommonly fine shit and snot!
　　Now really, the two
　　Are too good to be true –
I would rather have et them than not.'

1879–1941

314

A Dutchman who dwelt in Dundee
Walked in to a grocer's named Lee.
    He said, 'If you blease
    Haff you any prick cheese?'
Said the grocer, 'I'll skin back and see.'

                      1941–1948

315

A coprophagous fellow named Fleam
Loved to drink a strong urinal stream.
    He seduced little gonsils
    Into spraying his tonsils
With the stuff he liked best on earth: cream.

                      1942

316

There was a young fellow named Fritz
Who planted an acre of tits.
    They came up in the fall,
    Pink nipples and all,
And he chewed them all up into bits.

                      1941

317

There was a young man of Glengarridge,
The fruit of a scrofulous marriage.
    He sucked off his brother,
    And buggered his mother,
And ate up his sister's miscarriage.

                      1934–1941

318

A daughter of fair Ioway,
While at sport in the toilet one day,
    Swallowed some of her pee,
    'And hereafter,' said she,
'I'll do it at lunch every day.'

                      1946A

319

A young lady who once had a Jew beau
Found out soon that he'd got a bubo,
   So when it was ripe
   She put in a pipe,
And sucked up the juice through a tube oh!

                1870

320

There was a young fellow of Kent
Who had a peculiar bent.
   He collected the turds
   Of various birds,
And had them for lunch during Lent.

                1947B

321

There was a young man of King's Cross
Who amused himself frigging a horse,
   Then licking the spend
   Which still dripped from the end,
Said, 'It tastes just like anchovy sauce.'

                1879

322

A hypocritical bastard named Legman
When drinking piss-highballs puts egg in 'em.
   If he tells you you're queer
   To enjoy pissless beer,
Just say to him, 'Quit pulling my leg, man!'

                1952

323

There was a young fellow from Leith
Who used to skin cocks with his teeth.
   It wasn't for pleasure
   He adopted this measure,
But to get at the cheese underneath.

            1934–1938

324

Said a busy young whore known as Mable,
Who at fucking was willing and able,
  'It's a pity to waste
  All that juicy white paste,'
So she served it in bowls at the table.

1942

325

There once was a U.S. marine
Whose manners were slightly obscene.
  He loved to eat jizz,
  Both others' and his,
When served in a hot soup-tureen.

1941*

326

There was a young man from Marseilles
Who lived on clap juice and snails.
  When tired of these
  He lived upon cheese
From his prick, which he picked with his nails.

1927

327

There was an old maid from Shalot
Who lived upon frog shit and snot.
  When she tired of these
  She would eat the green cheese
That she scraped from the sides of her twat.

1927–1943c

328

There was an old sailor named Jock
Who was wrecked on a desolate rock.
  He had nothing to eat
  But the punk of his feet,
And the cheese from the end of his cock.

1941

329

There once was a baker of Nottingham
Who in making éclairs would put snot in 'em.
   When he ran out of snot,
    He would, like as not,
Take his pecker and jack off a shot in 'em.

                                1941

330

There was a young fellow of Perth,
The nastiest bastard on earth,
   When his wife was confined
    He pulled down the blind,
And ate up the whole afterbirth.

                                1941

331

A mannerly fellow named Phyfe
Was greatly distressed by his wife,
   For whene'er she was able
    She'd shit on the table,
And gobble the shit – with her knife!

                              1944A

332

There were two little mice in Rangoon
Who sought lunch in an old lady's womb.
   Cried one mouse, 'By Jesus,
    I'll wager this cheese is
As old as the cheese in the moon!'

                                1941

333

Where was a young lady of Rheims
Who was terribly plagued with wet dreams.
   She saved up a dozen,
    And sent to her cousin,
Who ate them and thought they were creams.

                                1879

334

An elderly rabbi named Riskin
Dines daily on cunt-juice and foreskin.
   And to further his bliss,
   At dessert he'll drink piss,
For which he is always a'thirstin'.

1946A

335

There was a young man known as Royce
Who took an emetic by choice.
   He was fed, quite by chance,
   Half the crotch of the pants
Of a girl who kept crab-lice as toys.

1942–1952

336

There was a young man of St. Just
Who ate of new bread till he bust.
   It was not the crumb,
   For that passed through his bum,
But what buggered him up was the crust.

1870

337

There was an old man of Seringapatam
Besmeared his wife's anus with raspberry jam,
   Then licked off the sweet,
   And pronounced it a treat,
And for public opinion he cared not a damn.

1870

338

There was a young lady of Totten
Whose tastes grew perverted and rotten.
   She cared not for steaks,
   Or for pastry and cakes,
But lived upon penis *au gratin.*

1938

339

There was a young man of the Tweed
Who sucked his wife's arse thro' a reed.
   When she had diarrhoea
   He'd let none come near,
For fear they should poach on his feed.

1879

340

There was a young pair from Uganda
Who were having a fuck on a veranda.
   The drip from their fucks
   Fed forty-two ducks,
Three geese, and a fucking big gander.

1942

341

A hungry old trollop from Yemen
Did a pretty good business with he-men.
   But she gave up all fucking
   In favor of sucking,
For the protein contained in the semen.

1947B

V PROSTITUTION

342

There once was a girl from Alaska
Who would fuck whenever you'd ask her.
  But soon she grew nice
  And went up in price,
And no one could touch her but Jesus H. Christ,
Or possibly John Jacob Astor.

1927–1932

343

A vicious old whore of Albania
Hated men with a terrible mania.
  With a twitch and a squirm
  She would hold back your sperm,
And then roll on her face and disdain ya.

1941

344

There was an old whore of Algiers
Who had bushels of dirt in her ears.
  The tip of her titty
  Was also quite shitty,
She never had washed it in years.

1938–1941

345

A guy met a girl in Anacostia
And said, 'Darling, dare I accost ya?
  I got only a buck,
  Is that good for a fuck?'
She replied, 'Not a fart will it cost ya.'

1943

346

There once was a floozie named Annie
Whose prices were cosy – but canny:
   A buck for a fuck,
   Fifty cents for a suck,
And a dime for a feel of her fanny.

1943B

347

Said an elderly whore named Arlene,
'I prefer a young lad of eighteen.
   There's more cream in his larder,
   And his pecker gets harder,
And he fucks in a manner obscene.'

1942

348

When the Duchess of Bagliofuente
Took her fourteenth *cavaliere servente*,
   The Duke said, 'Old chappy,
   I'll keep that quim happy
If I have to hire nineteen or twenty.'

1942A

349

There was a young man from Berlin,
A patron of sexual sin,
   He crammed the small crease
   'Twixt the legs of his niece
With a foot of his old rolling pin.

1945

350

There was a young chip from Brazil
Who fucked like a veritable mill.
   There was never a whore,
   When she'd finished her chore,
More prompt to present you her bill.

1942

351

There was a young trucker named Briard
Who had a young whore that he hired
   To fuck when not trucking,
   But trucking *plus* fucking
Got him so fucking tired he got fired.

1941

352

There was a young fellow called Cary,
Who got fucking the Virgin Mary.
   And Christ was so bored
   At seeing Ma whored
That he set himself up as a fairy.

1928

353

There once was a girl from the chorus
Whose virtue was known to be porous.
   She started by candling,
   And ended by handling
The whole clientèle of a whorehouse.

1943B

354

A hard-working waitress named Cora
Discovered that drummers adore a
   Titty that's ripe
   And a cunt that is tripe –
Now she doesn't work hard any more-a!

1941

355

A lady named Belle da Cunt Corrigan
Was the mistress of J. Pierpont Morigan,
   Till she handed the banker
   A hell of a chancre,
And now she is just a plain whore again.

1941

356

There was a young harlot of Crete
Whose fucking was far, far too fleet.
    So they tied down her ass
    With a long ton of brass
To give them a much longer treat.

When the Nazis landed in Crete
This young harlot had to compete
    With the many Storm Troopers
    Who were using their poopers
For other things than to excrete.

Our subversive young harlot of Crete
Was led to fifth-column deceit.
    When the paratroops landed
    Her trade she expanded
By at once going down on their meat.

Then here was this harlot of Crete,
She decided to be very neat.
    She said, 'I'm too high class
    To ream common ass,
And I'll wash every prick that I eat.'

And at last this fine harlot of Crete
Was hawking her meat in the street.
    Ambling out one fine day
    In a casual way,
She clapped up the whole British fleet.

                                    1943–1951

361

There was a young lady from Cue
Who filled her vagina with glue.
    She said with a grin,
    'If they pay to get in,
They'll pay to get out of it too.'

1947B

362

There was a young girl named Dale
Who put up her ass for sale.
    For the sum of two bits
    You could tickle her tits,
But a buck would get you real tail.

1942

363

To succeed in the brothels at Derna
One always begins as a learner.
    Indentured at six
    As a greaser of pricks,
One may rise to be fitter and turner.

1946B

364

There was a young girl from Des Moines
Who had a large sack full of coins.
    The nickels and dimes
    She got from the times
That she cradled the boys in her loins.

1945

365

A passion-swept dame called Dolores
Is the hottest of history's whores.
    Though we fuck her with zest,
    When we crawl home to rest,
Guess who's there waiting for us –
    Dolores, of cour-es!

1941

366

A young man, quite free with his dong,
Said the thing could be had for a song.
  Such response did he get
  That he rented the Met,
And held auditions all the day long.

1942

367

A sempstress at Epping-on-Tyne
Used to peddle her tail down the line.
  She first got a crown,
  But her prices went down –
Now she'll fit you for ten pence or nine.

1942A

368

There was a young lady of Erskine,
And the chief of her charms was her fair skin,
  But the sable she wore
  (She had several more)
She had earned while wearing her bare skin.

1941

369

Two young girls who lived in Ft. Tunney
Decided to shop their dofunny.
  'We had papa tutor us
  To cash in on our uterus;
We park transients now, in each cunny!'

1943B

370

Said the whore whom they called Geraldine,
'When I think of the pricks that I've seen,
  And all of the nuts
  And the ass-holes and butts,
And the bastards like you in between . . .'

1942–1952

371

A notorious whore named Miss Hearst
In the weakness of men is well versed.
   Reads a sign o'er the head
   Of her well-rumpled bed:
'The customer always comes first.'

1945

372

Said a pretty young whore of Hong Kong
To a long-pronged patron named Wong,
   'They say my vagina's
   The nicest in China –
Don't ruin it by donging it wrong.'

1941

373

There was a young man of Jaipur
Whose cock was shot off in the War.
   So he painted the front
   To resemble a cunt,
And set himself up as a whore.

1938

374

Since donning a uniform, Joe
Quit the floozies that he used to know.
   Says he, 'Joan Bennett'll
   Tickle my genital
Every night at the old U.S.O.'

1944

375

A shiftless young fellow of Kent
Had his wife fuck the landlord for rent.
   But as she grew older
   The landlord grew colder,
And now they live out in a tent.

1941

376

There was an old girl of Kilkenny
Whose usual charge was a penny.
　　For the half of that sum
　　You could finger her bum –
A source of amusement to many.

1928–1947B

377

Said a madam named Mamie La Farge
To a sailor just off a barge,
　　'We have one girl that's dead,
　　With a hole in her head –
Of course there's a slight extra charge.'

1944A

378

Have you heard about Dorothy Lamour,
Whose lovers got fewer and fewer?
　　When asked why she lost 'em
　　She said, 'I defrost 'em –
I guess I'm not made for a whore.'

1942–1952

379

In the city of York there's a lass
Who will hitch up her dress when you pass.
　　If you toss her two bits
　　She will strip to the tits,
And let you explore her bare ass.

1945

380

A harlot of note named Le Dux
Would always charge seventy bucks.
　　But for that she would suck you,
　　And wink-off and fuck you –
The whole thing was simple de luxe!

1941

381

There was an old hag named Le Sueur
Who just was an out-and-out whore.
  Between her big teats
  You could come for two bits,
And she'd fuck in any old sewer.

1946A

382

Any whore whose door sports a red light
Knows a prick when she sees one, all right.
  She can tell by a glance
  At the drape of men's pants
If they're worth taking on for the night.

1943

383

There was a young lady named Mable
Who would fuck on a bed or a table.
  Though a two-dollar screw
  Was the best she could do,
Her ass bore a ten-dollar label.

1944–1952

384

There was a young whore from Madrid
Who anyone could fuck for a quid.
  But a bastard Italian
  With balls like a stallion
Said he'd do it for nothing – and did.

1938

385

Les cocottes de la ville de Marseille
Sont brunettes de l'ardent soleil.
  Elles pissent du vin blanc,
  Couchent pour dix francs –
Mais où sont les patentes de santé?

1942A

386

The tarts in the town of Marseilles
Are brunette from the sun every day.
  White wine is their piddle,
  For ten francs they'll diddle –
But their tickets of health, where are they?

1942A

387

Unique is a strumpet of Mazur
In the way that her clientèle pays her:
  A machine that she uses
  Clamps on to her whoosis,
And clocks everybody that lays her.

1941

388

There was an old whore named McGee
Who was just the right sort for a spree.
  She said, 'For a fuck
  I charge half a buck,
And I throw in the ass-hole for free.'

1944A

389

Said a dainty young whore named Miss Meggs,
'The men like to spread my two legs,
  Then slip in between,
  If you know what I mean,
And leave me the white of their eggs.'

1943

390

Said a naked young soldier named Mickey
As his cunt eyed his stiff, throbbing dickey,
  'Kid, my leave's almost up,
  But I feel like a tup;
Bend down, and I'll slip you a quickie.'

1951

391

A school marm from old Mississippi
Had a quim that was simply zippy.
   The scholars all praised it
   Till finally she raised it
To prices befitting a chippy.

1952

392

There was a young thing from Missouri
Who fancied herself as a houri.
   Her friends thus forsook her,
   For a harlot they took her,
And she gave up the role in a fury.

1952

393

There was a young lady named Moore
Who, while not quite precisely a whore,
   Couldn't pass up a chance
   To take down her pants,
And compare some man's stroke with her bore.

1941

394

A tired young trollop of Nome
Was worn out from her toes to her dome.
   Eight miners came screwing,
   But she said, 'Nothing doing;
One of you has to go home!'

1941

395

There was a young woman of Norway
Who drove a rare trade in the whore way,
   Till a sodomite Viscount
   Brought cunt to a discount,
And the bawdy house belles to a poor way.

1870*

396

Said Clark Gable, picking his nose,
'I get more than the public suppose.
   Take the Hollywood way,
   It's the women who pay,
And the men simply take off their clothes.'

1939A

397

A chippy whose name was O'Dare
Sailed on a ship to Kenmare,
   But this cute little honey
   Had left home her money
So she laid the whole crew for her fare.

1946A

398

A sailor ashore in Peru
Said, 'Signora, quanto por la screw?'
   'For only one peso
   I will, if you say so,
Be buggered and nibble it too.'

1942A

399

A sprightly young tart in Pompeii
Used to make fifty drachma per lay.
   But age dimmed her renown
   And now she lies down
Fifty times for the same pay.

1942A

400

A soi-disant Mynheer Professor
Met a beat-up old whore from Odessa.
   She applied all her arts
   To his genital parts,
But they only grew lesser and lesser.

1948A

401

Says a busy young whore named Miss Randalls,
As men by the dozens she handles,
   'When I get this busy
   My cunt gets all jizzy,
And it runs down my legs like wax candles.'

1942

402

A whorehouse at 9 rue de Rennes
Had trouble in luring in men,
   Till they got some fairies
   With pretty dillberries,
And their clientèle came back again.

1942A

403

There was a young lady in Reno
Who lost all her dough playing keeno.
   But she lay on her back
   And opened her crack,
And now she owns the casino.

1942

404

A prosperous merchant of Rhône
Took orders for cunt on the phone,
   Or the same could be baled,
   Stamped, labeled, and mailed
To a limited parcel-post zone.

DuPont, I. G. Monsanto, and Shell
Built a world-circling pussy cartel,
   And by planned obsolescence
   So controlled detumescence
A poor man could not get a smell.

1948A

406

There was a rich old roué
Who felt himself slipping away.
   He endowed a large ward
   In a house where he'd whored.
Was there a crowd at his funeral? I'll say!

1948

407

There was a hot girl from the Saar
Who fucked all, both from near and from far.
   When asked to explain,
   She replied with disdain,
'I'm trying to buy me a car.'

1943

408

There was a young girl from St. Cyr
Whose reflex reactions were queer.
   Her escort said, 'Mabel,
   Get up off the table;
That money's to pay for the beer.'

1949

409

A licentious old justice of Salem
Used to catch all the harlots and jail 'em.
   But instead of a fine
   He would stand them in line,
With his common-law tool to impale 'em.

1941

410

There was an old girl of Silesia
Who said, 'As my cunt doesn't please ya,
   You might as well come
   Up my slimy old bum
But be careful my tapeworm don't seize ya.'

1927–1941

411

Ethnologists up with the Sioux
Wired home for two punts, one canoe.
    The answer next day
    Said, 'Girls on the way,
But what the hell's a "panoe"?'

1946A

412

There was a young lady from Slough
Who said that she didn't know how.
    Then a young fellow caught her
    And jolly well taught her;
She lodges in Pimlico now.

1928

413

Said a girl from Staraya Russa,
Whom the war had made looser and looser,
    'Yes, I'm wormin' a German,
    A vermin named Hermann,
But his dink is a lollapalooza!'

1942

414

There was an old Count of Swoboda
Who would not pay a whore what he owed her.
    So with great *savoir-faire*
    She stood on a chair,
And pissed in his whiskey-and-soda.

1938–1941

415

There was an old man of Tagore
Who tried out his cook as a whore
    He used Bridget's twidget
    To fidget his digit,
And now she won't cook any more.

1941

416

There was a young whore from Tashkent
Who managed an immoral tent.
   Day out and day in
   She lay writhing in sin,
Giving thanks it was ten months to Lent.

1946B

417

A young girl who was no good at tennis,
But at swimming was really a menace,
   Took pains to explain,
   'It depends how you train:
I was a street-walker in Venice.'

1946

418

There was a young man from the War Office
Who got into bed with a whore of his.
   She took off her drawers
   With many a pause,
But the chap from the War Office tore off his.

1938

419

There was an old whore of Warsaw
Who fucked all her customers raw.
   She would thump with her rump,
   And punt with her cunt,
And lick every prick that she saw.

1941

420

There once was a knowledgeful whore
Who knew all the coital lore.
   But she found there were many
   Who preferred her fat fanny,
And now she don't fuck any more.

1948A

421

There once was a versatile whore,
As expert behind as before.
   For a quid you could view her,
   And bugger and screw her,
As she stood on her head on the floor.

1941

422

There was an old harlot of Wick
Who was sucking a coal-heaver's prick.
   She said, 'I don't mind
   The coal-dust and grime,
But the smell of your balls makes me sick.'

1882–1941

423

There once was a harlot at Yale
With her price-list tattooed on her tail,
   And on her behind,
   For the sake of the blind,
She had it embroidered in Braille.

1941

VI DISEASES

424

Remember those two of Aberystwyth
Who connected the things that they pissed with?
   She sat on his lap
   But they both had the clap,
And they cursed with the things that they kissed
   with.   1928B–1944A

425

A sultan named Abou ben Adhem
Thus cautioned a travelling madam,
   'I suffer from crabs
   As do most us A-rabs,'
'It's all right,' said the madam, 'I've had
   'em.'   1946A

426

There was an old whore of Azores
Whose cunt was all covered with sores.
   The dogs in the street
   Wouldn't eat the green meat
That hung in festoons from her drawers.
                     1941

427

There was a young fellow – a banker,
Had bubo, itch, pox, and chancre.
   He got all the four
   From a dirty old whore,
So he wrote her a letter to thank her.
               1911–1927

428   LUETIC LAMENT

There was a young man of Back Bay
Who thought syphilis just went away,
  And felt that a chancre
  Was merely a canker
Acquired in lascivious play.

Now first he got acne vulgaris,
The kind that is rampant in Paris,
  It covered his skin,
  From forehead to shin,
And now people ask where his hair is.

With symptoms increasing in number,
His aorta's in need of a plumber,
  His heart is cavorting,
  His wife is aborting,
And now he's acquired a gumma.

Consider his terrible plight –
His eyes won't react to the light,
  His hands are apraxic,
  His gait is ataxic,
He's developing gun-barrel sight.

His passions are strong, as before,
But his penis is flaccid, and sore,
  His wife now has tabes
  And sabre-shinned babies –
She's really worse off than a whore.

There are pains in his belly and knees,
His sphincters have gone by degrees,
   Paroxysmal incontinence,
   With all its concomitants,
Brings on quite unpredictable pees.

Though treated in every known way,
His spirochetes grow day by day,
   He's developed paresis,
   Converses with Jesus,
And thinks he's the Queen of the May.

1938–1941

435

There was a young girl of Bavaria
Who thought her disease was malaria.
   But the family doc
   Remarked to her shock,
'It is in the mercurial area.'

1941

436

A noble young lord named Bellasis
Was a sad case of satyriasis,
   Till help psychiatric
   Brought the fucking fanatic
To a state of sexual stasis.

1947B

437

There was a young man of Berlin
Whom disease had despoiled of his skin,
   But he said with much pride,
   'Though deprived of my hide,
I can still enjoy a put in.'

1879

438

There was a young man of Cashmere
Who purchased a fine Bayadere.
  He fucked all her toes,
   Her mouth, eyes, and her nose,
And eventually poxed her left ear.

1879

439

There was a young woman of Cheadle
Who once gave the clap to a beadle.
  Said she, 'Does it itch?'
   'It does, you damned bitch,
And burns like hell-fire when I peedle.'

1879

440

There was a young woman of Chester
Who said to the man who undressed her,
  'I think you will find
   That it's better behind –
The front is beginning to fester.'

1927–1941

441

There was an old sarge of Dorchester
Who invented a mechanical whore-tester.
  With an electrical eye,
   His tool, and a die,
He observed each sore pimple and fester.

1944

442

There's a man in the city of Dublin
Whose pego is always him troubling,
  And it's now come to this,
   That he can't go to piss,
But the spunk with the piddle comes bubbling.

1870

443

There was a young priest of Dundee
Who went back of the parish to pee.
   He said, '*Pax vobiscum,*
    Why doesn't the piss come?
I must have the c-l-a-p.'

                       1928*–1941

444

There was an old party of Fife
Who suspected a clap in his wife.
   So he bought an injection
    To cure the infection,
Which gave him a stricture for life.

                       1870

445

There was a young rounder named Fisk
Whose method of screwing was brisk.
   And his reason was: 'If
    The damned bitch has the syph,
This way I'm reducing the risk.'

                       1941

446

A horny young soldier named Frank
Had only his girl-friend to thank
   That he didn't catch clap,
    Gonorrhea or pap,
And wind up in an oxygen tank.

                       1943

447

A president called Gambetta
Once used an imperfect French Letter.
   This was not the worst,
    With disease he got cursed,
And he took a long time to get better.

                       1879

448

There was a young lady of Gaza
Who shaved her cunt clean with a razor.
   The crabs in a lump
   Made tracks to her rump,
Which proceeding did greatly amaze her.

1879

449

There was an old man of Goditch,
Had the syph and the clap and the itch.
   His name was McNabs
   And he also had crabs,
The dirty old son of a bitch.

1927–1941

450

There was a young lady from Ipswich
Who had syphilis, pox, and the itch.
   In her box she put pepper
   And slept with a leper,
And ruined that son of a bitch.

1945c

451

A lecherous fellow named Gould
Soliloquized thus to his tool:
   'From Cape Cod to Salamanca,
   You've had pox, clap, and chancre –
Now ain't you a bloody great fool?'

1939A–1946B

452

There was a young lady of Grotton
Had to plug up her coosie with cotton,
   For it was no myth
   That the girl had the syph –
She stunk, and her titties were rotten.

1941

453

There was a young woman of Hadley
Who would with an omnibus cad lie.
   He gave her the crabs,
   And besides minor scabs
The pox too she got very badly.

1870

454

A strapping young fellow named Herman
Had a ring round his prick that was permanent.
   All the old docs
   Said the ring was the pox,
But he swore it was lipstick or vermin.

1941

455

There was a young lady named Hitchin
Who was scratching her crotch in the kitchen.
   Her mother said, 'Rose,
   It's the crabs, I suppose.'
She said, 'Yes, and the buggers are itchin'.'

1879–1941

456

Young Tom Doane, a promising jockey,
Laid up his spurs, feeling rocky.
   'I have got saddle-galls
   On both of my balls.'
But the doctor wrote down: Gonococci.

1942A

457

There was a young girl of Kilkenny
On whose genital parts there were many
   Venereal growths –
   The result of wild oats
Sown there by a fellow named Benny.

1946A

458

There was a young maid of Klepper
Went out one night with a stepper,
    And now in dismay
    She murmurs each day,
'His pee-pee was made of red-pepper!'

1927

459

The physicians of Countess van Krapp
Found a terrible rash on her map –
    Sores that opened and closed
    Which they soon diagnosed
As a case of perennial clap.

1941

460

There was a young lady named Lea
Whose favors were frequent and free,
    And pants-pigeons flew
    Where her goose-berries grew,
And some of them flew onto me.

1944A

461

He'll be there to inspect me,
With a big syringe to inject me –
    Oh, I'll be humpbacked
    Before I get back
To Ten-Ten-Tennessee . . .

1919–1939*

462

There was a young lady of Michigan
Who said, 'Damn it! I've got the itch again.'
    Said her mother, 'That's strange,
    I'm surprised it ain't mange,
If you've slept with that son-of-a-bitch-again.'

1941

463

There was an old man of Molucca
Who wanted his daughter, to fuck her.
  But she got the best
  Of his little incest,
And poxed the old man of Molucca.

1870

464

There was a young lady named Nance
Who had ants in the seat of her pants.
  When they bit her on bottom
  She yelled, 'Jesus God rot 'em!
I can't do the St. Vitus dance.'

1942–1952

465

There once was a Spanish nobilio
Who lived in a Spanish castilio,
  His *cojones* grew hot
  Much more often than not,
At the thought of a Spanish jazzilio.

1941*

466

The wife of a Viking in Norway
Was caught taking a nap in a doorway.
  'When you make the attack,
  Let it be from the back,
Because lately the front way's the sore way.'

1942A

467

Alack, for the doughty O'Connor
Who fucked like a fiend for his honor,
  Till a flapper named Rhea
  Colluded to be a
Mother to Leuco and Gonor.

1942A

468

A charming young lady named Randall
Has a clap that the doctors can't handle.
   So this lovely, lorn floozie,
   With her poor, damaged coosie,
Must take her delight with a candle.

1941

469

A rank whore, there ne'er was a ranker,
Possessed an Hunterian chancre,
   But she made an elision
   By a transverse incision,
For which all her lovers may thank her.

1870

470

There was a young lady of Reading,
Who got poxed, and the virus kept spreading.
   Her nymphae each day
   Kept sloughing away,
Till at last you could shove your whole head in.

1882

471

A girl to the druggist did say,
'I am bothered with bugs in my hay.'
   'I see what you mean,
   You need Paris green
To be rid of the things right away.'

The results of this piece of mischance
Were disastrous, you'll see at a glance.
   First died bugs, then went trees,
   Then her pet Pekinese,
And two gentlemen just in from France.

1948A

473

There was a young lady at sea
Who said, 'God, how it hurts me to pee.'
   'I see,' said the mate,
   'That accounts for the state
Of the captain, the purser, and me.'

                     1925*–1927

474

A virile young G.I. named Shorty
Was lively, and known to be 'sporty'.
   But he once made a slip
   And showed up with a 'drip',
And was red-lined (35–1440).

                     1943

475

A boy whose skin long I suppose is,
Was dreadfully ill with phymosis.
   The doctor said, 'Why,
   Circumcision we'll try,
A plan recommended by Moses.'

                     1870

476

There was an old man of Tantivy
Who followed his son to the privy.
   He lifted the lid
   To see what he did,
And found that it smelt of Capivi.

                     1879

477

There was an old man at the Terminus
Whose bush and whose bum were all verminous.
   They said, 'You *sale Boche!*
   You really must wash
Before you start planting your sperm in us.'

                     1928

478

There was a young girl of Uttoxeter,
And all the young men shook their cocks at her.
  From one of these cocks
  She contracted the pox,
And she poxed all the cocks in Uttoxeter.

1870–1941

479

A fellow who slept with a whore
Used a safe, but his pecker got sore.
  Said he with chagrin,
  'Selling these is a sin.'
Said the druggist, '*Caveat emptor*.'

1946

480

Full ninety years old was friend Wynn
When he went to a hookshop to sin.
  But try as he would
  It did him no good.
For all he had left was the skin.

1927–1948

481

There was a young lady of Yap
Who had pimples all over her map.
  But in her interstices
  There lurked a far worse disease,
Commonly known as the clap.

1947B

VII LOSSES

NOTE

[*Losses through the agency of animals
will be found in Chapter III, 'Zoophily'.*

*Losses in connection with masturbation
will be found in Chapter VIII, 'Sex Substitutes'.*]

482

There was a young lady of Alnwicke
Whom a stranger threw into a panic.
  For he frigged her and fucked her,
  And buggered and sucked her,
With a glee hardly short of satanic.

1941

483

I lost my arm in the army,
I lost my leg in the navy,
  I lost my balls
  Over Niagara Falls,
And I lost my cock in a lady.

1939*

484

An explorer returned from Australia,
Reported lost paraphernalia:
  A Zeiss microscope
  And his personal hope,
Which had vanished with his genitalia.

1942A

485

There was a young sailor named Bates
Who did the fandango on skates.
  He fell on his cutlass
  Which rendered him nutless
And practically useless on dates.

1944–1952

486

There was an old maid from Bermuda
Who shot a marauding intruder.
  It was not her ire
  At his lack of attire,
But he reached for her jewels as he screwed her.

1950

487

There was a young fellow named Bill
Who took an atomic pill.
  His navel corroded,
  His asshole exploded,
And they found his nuts in Brazil.

1948

488

While pissing on deck, an old boatswain
Fell asleep, and his pisser got frozen.
  It snapped at the shank,
  And it fell off and sank
In the sea – 'twas his own fault for dozin'.

1941

489

There was a young fellow named Bob
Who explained to his friends with a sob,
  'The size of my phallus
  Was just right for Alice
Till the night that she bit off the knob.'

1941

490

There was a young fellow from Boston
Who rode around in an Austin.
   There was room for his ass
   And a gallon of gas,
But his balls hung outside, and he lost 'em.

1938

491

A miner who bored in Brazil
Found some very strange rust on his drill.
   He thought it a joke
   Till the bloody thing broke –
Now his tailings are practically nil.

1942A

492

An eccentric young poet named Brown
Raised up his embroiderèd gown
   To look for his peter
   To beat it to metre,
But fainted when none could be found.

1941A

493

A Bavarian dame named Brunhilde
Went to bed with a jerry-built builder.
   The end of his john
   Was so badly put on
That it snapped in her bladder and killed her.

1941

494

There was a young man of Calcutta
Who tried to write 'Cunt' on a shutter.
   He had got to 'C-U-'
   When a pious Hindu
Knocked him arse over tip in the gutter.

1879–1928

495

There was a young man of Canute
Who was troubled by warts on his root.
   He put acid on these,
   And now, when he pees,
He can finger his root like a flute.

1941

496

Another young man, from Beirut
Played a penis as one might a flute,
   Till he met a sad eunuch
   Who lifted his tunic
And said, 'Sir, my instrument's mute.'

1947B

497

There was a young girl in a cast
Who had an unsavory past,
   For the neighborhood pastor
   Tried fucking through plaster,
And his very first fuck was his last.

1948A

498

There were two young men of Cawnpore
Who buggered and fucked the same whore.
   But the partition split
   And the gism and shit
Rolled out in great lumps on the floor.

1928–1949

499

The wife of a red-headed Celt
Lost the key to her chastity-belt.
   She tried picking the lock
   With an Ulsterman's cock,
And the next thing he knew, he was gelt.

1944

500

There was an old lady of Cheadle
Who sat down in church on a needle.
   The needle, though blunt,
   Penetrated her cunt,
But was promptly removed by the beadle.

1879–1941

501

The wife of an athlete named Chuck
Found her married life shit-out-of-luck.
   Her husband played hockey
   Without wearing a jockey –
Now he hasn't got what it takes for a fuck.

1941*–1952

502

There was a young lady of Clewer
Who was riding a bike, and it threw her.
   A man saw her there
   With her legs in the air,
And seized the occasion to screw her.

1941

503

There was a young man of Coblenz
The size of whose balls was immense.
   One day, playing soccer,
   He sprung his left knocker,
And kicked it right over the fence.

1941

504

An unfortunate bugger named Cowl
Took a shit while as drunk as an owl.
   He stumbled, alack!
   And fell flat on his back,
And his ballocks slipped into his bowel.

1941

505

There was a young girl from the Creek
Who had her periods twice every week.
  'How very provoking,'
  Said the Vicar from Woking,
'There's no time for poking, so to speak.'

                     1927–1945c

506

The wife of a chronic crusader
Took on every man who waylaid her.
  Till the amorous itch
  Of this popular bitch
So annoyed the crusader he spayed her.

                     1942

507

There was a young lady of Dee
Who went down to the river to swim.
  A man in a punt
  Stuck an oar in her eye,
And now she wears glasses, you see.

                  1941A–1948A

508

There was a young fellow named Dick
Who was cursed with a spiralling prick,
  So he set out to hunt
  For a screw-twisted cunt
That would match with his corkscrewy dick.

He found one, and took it to bed,
And then in chagrin he dropped dead,
  For that spiralling snatch
  It never would match –
The damn thing had a left-handed thread!

                  1934*–1941

510

There was a young girl named Dinwiddie
With a brace of voluptuous titty.
   But the boys squeezed them so
   That they hung down below,
And one drooped behind and got shitty.

1941

511

There was a young lady named Dowd
Whom a young fellow groped in the crowd.
   But the thing that most vexed her
   Was that when he stood next her
He said, 'How's your cunt?' right out loud.

1941

512

There was a young lady named Duff
With a lovely, luxuriant muff.
   In his haste to get in her
   One eager beginner
Lost both of his balls in the rough.

1941

513

There was a young lady named Eva
Who went to a ball as Godiva.
   But a change in the lights
   Showed a tear in her tights,
And a low fellow present yelled, 'Beaver!'

1927–1941

514

There was an old fellow of Ewing
Who said, 'It's computing I'm doing.
   By leaving my drawers on
   While clambering whores, on
The whole I've lost ten miles of screwing.'

1946A

515

There was a man from Far Rockaway
Who could skizzle a broad from a block away.
  Once while taking a fuck,
  Along came a truck
And knocked both his balls and his cock away.

1945c

516

There was a young fellow named Förster
Who fucked a young girl till he burst 'er.

[*The only two-line limerick.*]

1947b

517

And then there's a story that's fraught
With disaster – of balls that got caught,
  When a chap took a crap
  In the woods, and a trap
Underneath . . . Oh, I can't bear the thought!

1941

518

A careless old hooker in Frisco
Got turpentine mixed in her pisco
  And scalded with steam
  A muff-diver's dream
Because he refused to let puss go.

1942a

519

There was a young man from Glenchasm
Who had a tremendous orgasm.
  In the midst of his thralls
  He burst both his balls
And covered an acre with plasm.

1943a

520

There was an old person of Gosham
Who took out his ballocks to wash 'em.
  His wife said, 'Now, Jack,
  If you don't put them back,
I'll step on your scrotum and squash 'em.'
                     1938–1941

521

A gallant young Frenchman named Grandhomme
Was attempting a girl on a tandem.
  At the height of the make
  She slammed on the brake,
And scattered his semen at random.
                     1938

522

There was a young lady named Hall,
Wore a newspaper dress to a ball.
  The dress caught on fire
  And burned her entire
Front page, sporting section, and all.
                     1941

523

There was an old sheik named Al Hassid
Whose tool had become very placid.
  Before each injection
  To get an erection
He had to immerse it in acid.
                     1949

524

There was a young man in Havana,
Fucked a girl on a player piano.
  At the height of their fever
  Her ass hit the lever –
Yes! He has no banana!
                     1941

525   ANNE COOPER HEWITT

I'm only a sterilized heiress,
A butt for the laughter of rubes.
   I'm comely and rich
   But a venomous bitch –
My mother – ran off with my tubes.

Oh, fie on you mother, you dastard!
Come back with my feminine toys.
   Restore my abdomen
   And make me a woman –
I want to go out with the boys!

Imagine my stark consternation
At feeling a surgeon's rude hands
   Exploring my person
   (Page Aimée McPherson)
And then rudely snatching my glands.

Oh, fie on you medical monsters!
How could you so handle my charms
   My bosom is sinking,
   My clitoris shrinking –
I need a strong man in my arms!

The butler and second-man snub me,
No more will they use my door key.
   The cook from Samoa
   Has spermatozoa –
For others, but never for me.

Oh, fie on you fickle men-servants!
With your strong predilection to whore.
  Who cares for paternity?
  Forgive my infirmity –
Can't a girl just be fun any more?

What ruling in court can repay me
For losing my peas-in-the-pod?
  My joyous fecundity's
  Turned to morbundity –
Like Pickford, I'll have to try God.

Oh, fie on you, courthouse and rulings!
I want my twin bubbles of jest.
  Take away my hot flashes
  And menopause rashes,
And let me feel weight on my chest!

                                        1938*–1946A

533

There was a young man with a hernia
Who said to his surgeon, 'Gol-dernya,
  When carving my middle
  Be sure you don't fiddle
With matters that do not concernya.'

                                        1870–1939*

534

A marine being sent to Hong Kong
Got his doctor to alter his dong.
  He sailed off with a tool
  Flat and thin as a rule –
When he got there he found he was wrong.

                                        1942A

535

There was a young fellow named Hyde
Who took a girl out for a ride.
  He mucked up her fuck-hole
  And fucked up her muck-hole,
And charged her two dollars beside.

1941

536

Consider the case of Charles the Insane
Who had a large cock and a very small brain.
  While fucking his sister
  He raised a large blister
On the tip of his whip and her pubic terrain.

1945

537

There was a young Scotchman named Jock
Who had the most horrible shock:
  He once took a shit
  In a leaf-covered pit,
And the crap sprung a trap on his cock.

1941

538

The Conquering Lion of Judah
Made a prayer to the statue of Buddha.
  'Oh, Idol,' he prayed,
  'May Il Duce be spayed,
And all his descendants be neuter!'

1946B

539

There was a young couple named Kelly
Who had to live belly to belly,
  Because once, in their haste,
  They used library paste
Instead of petroleum jelly.

1938

540

There was a young man of Khartoum
Who lured a poor girl to her doom.
   He not only fucked her,
   But buggered and sucked her –
And left her to pay for the room.

                                   1938

541

Said old Mr. Wellington Koo,
'Now what in the Hell shall I do?
   My wife is too hot,
   I can't fill up her slot –'
So he screwed her to bits trying to.

                                   1952

542

A crooner who lived in Lahore
Got his balls caught in a door.
   Now his mezzo soprano
   Is rather piano
Though he was a loud basso before.

                               1942A

543

There was a young Marquis of Landsdowne,
Who tried hard to keep his great stands down.
   Said he, 'But that I thought
   I should break it off short,
My penis I'd hold with both hands down.'

                               1870

544

Did you hear about young Henry Lockett?
He was blown down the street by a rocket.
   The force of the blast
   Blew his balls up his ass,
And his pecker was found in his pocket.

                               1946B

545

There was a young girl named Louise
With a marvelous vaginal squeeze.
　　She inspired such pleasure
　　In her lover's yard measure,
That she caused his untimely decease.

1941

546

There was a young man of Madras
Who was fucking a girl in the grass,
　　But the tropical sun
　　Spoiled half of his fun
By singeing the hair off his ass.

1928–1941

547

There was a young man of Malacca
Who always slept on his left knacker.
　　One Saturday night
　　He slept on his right,
And his knacker went off like a cracker.

1941

548

Growing tired of her husband's great mass,
A young bride inserted some glass.
　　The prick of her hubby
　　Is now short and stubby,
While the wife can now piss through her ass.

1941*

549

A girl of as graceful a mien
As ever in London was seen,
　　Stepped into a pub,
　　Hit her man with a club,
And razored to shreds his machine.

1946A

550

There was a young man of Missouri
Who fucked with a terrible fury,
    Till hauled into court
    For his besti-al sport,
And condemned by a poorly-hung jury.

1951

551

All winter the eunuch from Munich
Went walking in naught but a tunic.
    Folks said, 'You've a cough;
    You'll freeze your balls off!'
Said he, 'That's why I'm a eunuch.'

1939A

552

There was a young lady named Nance
Whose lover had St. Vitus dance.
    When she dove for his prick,
    He wriggled so quick,
She bit a piece out of his pants.

1941

553

There was a young lady in Natchez
Who fell in some nettle-wood patches.
    She sits in her room
    With her bare little moon,
And scratches, and scratches, and scratches.

1927

554

There was an old man from New York
Whose tool was as dry as a cork.
    While attempting to screw
    He split it in two,
And now his tool is a fork.

1952

555

A bridegroom at Niagara Falls,
His fate was sad, and it appalls:
  His bride refused to fuck him,
  Or bugger, frig, or suck him;
So he went nuts – cut off his putz,
  And then bit off his balls.

1941

556

When Abelard near Notre Dame
Had taught his fair pupil the game,
  Her uncle – the wag –
  Cut off Peter's bag,
And his lectures were never the same.

1942A

557

A young man of Novorossisk
Had a mating procedure so brisk,
  With such super-speed action
  The Lorentz contraction
Foreshortened his prick to a disk.

1946–1951*

558

There once was a Frenchman from Pau
Who went for a slide on the snow.
  He traveled so fast
  That he skinned off his ass,
And the cuticle now has to grow.

1940*–1946A

559

A nudist by name Roger Peet,
Loved to dance in the snow and the sleet,
  But one chilly December
  He froze every member,
And retired to a monkish retreat.

1939A

560

There was a young lady named Perkin
Who swallowed an extra-large gherkin.
  Now she doesn't spend much
  On kotex and such,
On account of her drain isn't workin'.

1941

561

There was a young man of Porcellian,
A rotter, a shit-heel, a hellion.
  But the X-ray revealed
  That his sperm was congealed,
And both of his balls in rebellion.

1941

562

A bibulous bishop would preach
After sunning his balls on the beach.
  But his love life was ended
  By a paunch so distended
It annulled, *ipso facto*, his reach.

1945

563

There was a young fellow named Puttenham
Whose tool caught in doors upon shuttin' 'em.
  He said, 'Well, perchance
  It would help to wear pants,
If I just could remember to button 'em.'

1949–1952

564

One evening a workman named Rawls
Fell asleep in his old overalls.
  And when he woke up he
  Discovered a puppy
Had bitten off both of his balls.

1941

565

A horny young fellow named Redge
Was jerking off under a hedge.
  The gardener drew near
  With a huge pruning shear,
And trimmed off the edge of his wedge.

1941

566

There once was a girl at the Ritz
Who liked to have men bite her tits.
  One good Fletcherizer
  Made her sadder but wiser
By chewing them up into bits.

1932–1941

567

A geologist named Dr. Robb
Was perturbed by his thingamabob,
  So he took up his pick
  And whanged off his wick.
And calmly went on with his job.

1942A

568

There was an old man from Robles
Who went out to dine with some nobles.
  He would risk his life,
  And fucked the host's wife,
And now, so 'tis said, he has no balls.

1927

569

When the White Man attempted to rule
The Indians made him a fool.
  They cut off his nuts
  To hang in their huts,
And stuffed up his mouth with his tool.

1943

570

There was a young singer named Springer,
Got his testicles caught in the wringer.
    He hollered with pain
    As they rolled down the drain,
(*falsetto*): 'There goes my career as a singer!'

1943

571

There was an old man of Stamboul
With a varicose vein in his tool.
    In attempting to come
    Up a little boy's bum
It burst, and he *did* look a fool.

1928

572

There was an old rake from Stamboul
Felt his ardor grow suddenly cool.
    No lack of affection
    Reduced his erection –
But his zipper got caught in his tool.

1943B

573

There was a young girl of high station
Who ruined her fine reputation
    When she said she'd the pox
    From sucking on cocks –
She should really have called it 'fellation'.

1941

574

When the Bermondsey bricklayers struck,
Bill Bloggins was 'aving a fuck.
    By uni-on rules
    He 'ad to down tools –
Now wasn't that bloody 'ard luck!

1947A

575

Said a doleful young man with a stutter,
'M-my wife don't allow me to butt her.
   It's-ts-ts-ts-'tsall right,
   B-b-but, but some night
I'll t-tie down the bitch, and g-gut her!'

A less violent chap with a stammer
Said, 'M-mine too – she won't let me ram her.
   What's s-soured me on life
   Is not f-fucking my wife,
D-d-d-d-d-d-d-d-dammer!'

                                   1941

577

There was a young man from Tahiti
Who went for a swim with his sweetie,
   And as he pursued her
   A blind barracuda
Ran off with his masculinity.

                                   1947

578

I'd rather have fingers than toes,
I'd rather have ears than a nose,
   And a happy erection
   Brought just to perfection
Makes me terribly sad when it goes.

                                 1948A

579

There was a young fellow named Tom
Who ran screaming home to his mom.
   The fear of the Bomb
   Scared him back in the womb –
The bastard, he wasn't so dumb!

                                 1950

580

There was a young lady of Tring
Who sat by the fire to sing.
   A piece of charcoal
   Flew up her arsehole
And burnt all the hair off her quim.

1870

581

There was a young man of Tyburnia
Who was fucking a girl with a hernia.
   When he shot in her twat
   Why, she also shot –
All over him! Wouldn't that burn ya?

1948A

582

An athletic young fellow in Venice
Got the stone from straining at tennis.
   When his jock wouldn't stand
   She who had it in hand
Said, 'These out-door sports are a menace.'

1942A

583

A lady was once heard to weep,
'My figure no more I can keep.
   It's my husband's demand
   For a tit in each hand,
But the bastard will walk in his sleep!'

1943A

584

There was a young lady of Wheeling
Who professed to lack sexual feeling.
   But a cynic named Boris
   Just touched her clitoris,
And she had to be scraped off the ceiling.

1941

585

There was a young lady named White
Found herself in a terrible plight:
  A mucker named Tucker
  Had struck her, the fucker –
The bugger, the bastard, the shite!

                         1927–1941

VIII SEX SUBSTITUTES

586

A man in the battle of Aix
Had one nut and his cock shot away,
  But found out in this pickle
  His nose could still tickle,
Though he might get the snuffles some day.

1942A

587

Nymphomaniacal Alice
Used a dynamite stick for a phallus.
  They found her vagina
  In North Carolina,
And her ass-hole in Buckingham Palace.

1942–1951

588

A lesbian lassie named Anny
Desired to appear much more manny.
  So she whittled a pud
  Of mahogany wood,
And let it protrude from her cranny.

1943A

589

There once was a young Aztec
Who was fond of reading Steinbeck.
  When asked where she read,
  She said, 'Always in bed,
Especially when wearing Ko-tex.'

1942

590

There was a young man of Bagdad
Who was dreaming that he was a shad.
   He dreamt he was spawning,
   And then, the next morning,
He found that, by Jesus! he had.

1944A

591

There was a young man of Balbriggan
Who was fearfully given to frigging,
   Till these nocturnal frolics
   Played hell with his bollox,
And killed the young man of Balbriggan.

1870

592

An eunuch frequenting Bangkok
Used to borrow the deified jock
   From a local rain-god
   When he went for a prod –
You could hear the girl yell for a block.

1942A

593

When a girl, young Elizabeth Barrett
Was found by her ma in a garret.
   She had shoved up a diamond
   As far as her hymen,
And was ramming it home with a carrot.

1932

594

There was a young girl of Batonger,
Used to diddle herself with a conger.
   When asked how it feels
   To be pleasured by eels,
She said, 'Just like a man, only longer.'

1941

595

A nudist resort at Benares
Took a midget in all unawares.
    But he made members weep
    For he just couldn't keep
His nose out of private affairs.

                                           1949

596

There was a young man from Bengal
Who got in a hole in the wall.
    'Oh,' he said, 'It's a pity
    This hole is so glitty,
But it's better than nothing at all.'

                                           1946a

597

There was an asexual bigot
Whose cock only served as a spigot,
    Till a jolly young whore
    Taught him tricks by the score;
Now his greatest delight is to frig it.

                                           1944

598

There once was a horny old bitch
With a motorized self-fucker which
    She would use with delight
    All day long and all night –
Twenty bucks: Abercrombie & Fitch.

                                           1941–1952

599

There was a young man of Bombay
Who fashioned a cunt out of clay,
    But the heat of his prick
    Turned it into a brick,
And chafed all his foreskin away.

                                           1879

600

A squeamish young fellow named Brand
Thought caressing his penis was grand,
   But he viewed with distaste
   The gelatinous paste
That it left in the palm of his hand.

1942

601

There was a young fellow named Bream
Who never had dreamt a wet dream,
   For when lacking a whore
   He'd just bore out the core
Of an apple, and fuck it through cream.

1941

602

There was a young man from the Bronx
Who when offered a piece said, 'No thonx.'
   He said, 'I declare,
   I prefer solitaire,
And all that I do is just yonx.'

1939A

603

There was a young naval cadet
Whose dreams were unusually wet.
   When he dreamt of his wedding
   He soaked up the bedding,
And the wedding ain't taken place yet.

1942–1952

604

There was a young man of Calcutta
Who jerked himself off in the gutter.
   But the tropical sun
   Played hell with his gun
And turned all his cream into butter.

1941–1951

605

A young jacker-off of Cawnpore
Never felt a desire for more.
   In bold self-reliance
   He cried out his defiance
Of the joys of the fairy and whore.

1942

606

There was a young fellow named Chisholm
Afflicted with skin erotism.
   In bathing, he'd rub
   His prick in the tub
Till the water was soapy with jism.

1942

607

There were two young ladies from Claversham
Who allowed two buck niggers to ravish 'em.
   Said May to Elize,
   'If we just close our eyes,
We'll imagine they're Hackett and Faversham!'

1943B

608

There was a young girl of Cohoes
Who jerked herself off with her nose.
   . She said, 'Yes, I done it,
   But just for the fun it
Afforded the folk of Cohoes.'

1952

609

There once was a fabulous Creole
Whose prick had a wide-open pee-hole.
   This carrot so orange
   Got caught in the door-hinge
When he tried to bugger the key-hole.

1941*

610

There was a young woman of Croft
Who played with herself in a loft,
   Having reasoned that candles
   Could never cause scandals,
Besides which they did not go soft.

1927–1949

611

Said another young woman of Croft,
Amusing herself in the loft,
   'A salami or wurst
   Is what I should choose first –
With bologna you know you've been boffed.'

1941–1952

612

There was a young lady of Dallas
Invented a singular phallus.
   It came and it went,
   And when it was spent
It proceeded to fill up the chalice.

1943A

613

There was a young fellow from Dallas
Who enjoyed doing things with his phallus.
   So many tricks did he try
   It became, by and by,
Little more than a leather-tough callus.

1943

614

There was a young man from Darjeeling
Whose dong reached up to the ceiling.
   In the electric light socket
   He'd put it and rock it –
Oh God! What a wonderful feeling!

1946A

615

A geneticist living in Delft
Scientifically played with himself,
   And when he was done
   He labeled it: *Son*,
And filed him away on a shelf.

1942A

616

A certain young fellow named Dick
Liked to feel a girl's hand on his prick.
   He taught them to fool
   With his rigid old tool
Till the cream shot out, white and thick.

1942

617

An agreeable girl named Miss Doves
Likes to jack off the young men she loves.
   She will use her bare fist
   If the fellows insist
But she really prefers to wear gloves.

1942

618

A lecherous Northumbrian druid,
Whose mind was filthy and lewd,
   Awoke from a trance
   With his hand in his pants
On a lump of pre-seminal fluid.

1945

619

There was an old Chinaman drunk
Who went for a sail in his junk.
   He was dreaming of Venus
   And tickling his penis,
Till he floated away in the spunk.

1879

620

There was a young man from Oswego
Who fell in love with a Dago.
   He dreamt that his Venus
   Was jerking his penis,
And woke up all covered with sago.

1946A

621

There was a gay Countess of Dufferin,
One night while her husband was covering,
   Just to chaff him a bit
   She said, 'You old shit,
I can buy a dildo for a sovereign.'

1870

622

The modern cinematic emporium
Is by no means the merest sexorium,
   But a highly effectual
   Heterosexual
Mutual masturbatorium.

1943*

623

As Apollo was chasing the fair
Daphne she vanished in air.
   He could find but a shrub
   With thick bark on the hub
And not even a knot-hole to spare.

1942A

624

There were three young ladies of Fetters,
Annoyed all their elders and betters
   By stuffing their cock-holders
   With proxies for stockholders,
Old bills, and anonymous letters.

1941

625

There was a young parson of Goring
Who made a small hole in the flooring.
    He lined it all round,
    Then laid on the ground,
And declared it was cheaper than whoring.

1879

626

A fair-haired young damsel named Grace
Thought it very, very foolish to place
    Her hand on your cock
    When it turned hard as rock,
For fear it would explode in her face.

1946A

627

There was a young lady of Harrow
Who complained that her cunt was too narrow,
    For times without number
    She would use a cucumber,
But could not accomplish a marrow.

1879

628

There was a young parson of Harwich,
Tried to grind his betrothed in a carriage.
    She said, 'No, you young goose,
    Just try self-abuse.
And the other we'll try after marriage.'

1879

629

There was a young lady named Hatch
Who doted on music by Bach.
    She played with her pussy
    To 'The Faun' by Debussy,
But to ragtime she just scratched her snatch.

1943–1952

630

There was a young man from Havana
Who continually played the 'piana'.
   'Til one day his finger slipped,
   And his fly it ripped,
And out slipped a hairy banana.

1950

631

A water-pipe suited Miss Hunt,
Who used it for many a bunt,
   But the unlucky wench
   Got it caught in her trench –
It took twenty-two men and a big Stillson wrench
To get the thing out of her cunt.

1941

632

At Vassar sex isn't injurious,
Though of love we are never penurious.
   Thanks to vulcanized aids
   Though we may die old maids,
At least we shall never die curious.

1941

633

The swaggering hips of a jade
Raised the cock of a clerical blade.
   Hell-bent for his fun
   He went home on the run,
And diddled his grandmother's maid.

1941

634

A neurotic young man of Kildare
Drilled a hole in the seat of a chair.
   He fucked it all night,
   Then died of the fright
That maybe he wasn't 'all there'.

1946A

635

There was a young lady from Kincaid
Who covered it up with a band-aid.
    The boy-friend said, 'Shit,
    I can't find the slit!'
And helped himself out with a hand-aid.

1948A

636

An amorous Jew, on Yom Kippur,
Saw a shiksel – decided to clip her.
    'I'll grip her, and strip her,
    And lip her, and whip her –'
Then his dingus shot off in his zipper!

1943B

637

There was a young fellow named Klotz
Who went looking for tail in New Lots.
    Of tail he found nary
    A piece, but a fairy
Suggested he try some ersatz.

1942–1947B

638

There was a young man of Kutki
Who could blink himself off with one eye.
    For a while though, he pined,
    When his organ declined
To function, because of a stye.

1947B

639

Since the girls found no joys in her lap,
Pete chopped off her big brother's tap.
    At his death she did not repent,
    But fixed it with cement
And wore it in place with a strap.

1942

640

An innocent boy in Lapland
Was told that frigging was grand.
    But at his first trial
    He said with a smile,
'I've had the same feeling by hand.'

1927

641

She made a thing of soft leather,
And topped off the end with a feather.
    When she poked it inside her
    She took off like a glider
And gave up her lover forever.

1948A

642

There is a young fellow from Leeds
Whose skin is so thin his cock bleeds
    Whenever erect,
    This dermal defect
Often scares him from sowing his seeds.

1947

643

There was a young fellow from Lees
Who handled his tool with great ease.
    This continual friction
    Made his sex a mere fiction,
But the callus hangs down to his knees.

1947

644

There was a young man from Liberia
Who was groping a wench from Nigeria.
    He said, 'Say, my pet,
    Your panties are wet.'
'Sorry, sir, that's my interior.'

1947B

645

There was a pianist named Liszt
Who played with one hand while he pissed,
   But as he grew older
   His technique grew bolder,
And in concert jacked off with his fist.

1941A

646

There was an old parson of Lundy,
Fell asleep in his vestry on Sunday.
   He awoke with a scream:
   'What, another wet dream!
This comes of not frigging since Monday.'

1879

647

A soldier named Dougall McDougall
Was caught jacking off in his bugle.
   Said they of the army,
   'We think that you're barmy,'
Said he, 'It's the new way to frugle.'

1939A

648

A thrifty old man named McEwen
Inquired, 'Why be bothered with screwing?
   It's safer and cleaner
   To finger your wiener,
And besides you can see what you're doing.'

1942A

649

There was a young man from McGill
Who was always seen walking uphill.
   When someone inquired,
   'My man, aren't you tired?'
He said, 'No, it makes my balls thrill.'

1939A

650

There was a young man named M'Gurk
Who dozed off one night after work,
   He had a wet dream
   But awoke with a scream
Just in time to give it a jerk.

1927–1941

651

Have you heard of Professor MacKay
Who lays all the girls in the hay?
   Though he thinks it's romantic
   He drives them all frantic
By *talking* a wonderful lay.

1942–1952

652

A horny young girl of Madras
Reclined with a monk in the grass.
   She tickled his cock
   With the end of a rock
Till it foamed like a bottle of Bass.

Another young lady named Hicks
Spent all her time thinking of pricks,
   And it was her odd whim
   To tickle her quim
Till it foamed like a bottle of Dicks.

1941–1951

654

A lusty young woodsman of Maine
For years with no woman had lain,
   But he found sublimation
   At a high elevation
In the crotch of a pine – God, the pain!

1941

655

There was a young lady named Mandel
Who caused quite a neighborhood scandal
  By coming out bare
  On the main village square
And frigging herself with a candle.

1943B

656

There was a young girl named Maxine
Whose vagina was wondrously clean:
  With her uterus packed
  She kept safe from attack
With a dill pickle, papulous, green.

1942A

657

There was a young lady named May
Who frigged herself in the hay.
  She bought a pickle –
  One for a nickel –
And wore all the warts away!

1927

658

In all of the Grecian metropolis
There was only one virgin – Papapoulos;
  But her cunt was all callous
  From fucking the phallus
Of a god that adorned the Acropolis.

1941

659

There were two Greek girls of Miletus
Who said, 'We wear gadgets that treat us,
  When strapped on the thigh
  Up cozy and high,
To constant, convenient coitus.'

1941

660

There was an aesthetic young Miss
Who thought it the apex of bliss
   To jazz herself silly
   With the bud of a lily,
Then go to the garden and piss.

1928

661

There was a young girl of Mobile
Whose hymen was made of chilled steel.
   To give her a thrill
   Took a rotary drill
Or a Number 9 emery wheel.

1938–1941

662

There was a young man from Montrose
Who could diddle himself with his toes.
   He did it so neat
   He fell in love with his feet,
And christened them Myrtle and Rose.

Oh, that supple young man of Montrose
Who tickled his tail with his toes!
   His landlady said,
   As she made up his bed,
'My God! How that man blows his nose!'

1927–1941

664

There was a young lady from Munich
Who was had in a park by a eunuch.
   In a moment of passion
   He shot her a ration
From a squirt-gun concealed 'neath his tunic.

1943A–1945

665

There was a young girl from New York
Who diddled herself with a cork.
 It stuck in her vagina –
 Can you imagina
Prying it out with a fork!

1938

666

There was a young man in Norway,
Tried to jerk himself off in a sleigh,
 But the air was so frigid
 It froze his balls rigid,
And all he could come was frappé.

1938–1941

667

A bobby of Nottingham Junction
Whose organ had long ceased to function
 Deceived his good wife
 For the rest of her life
With the aid of his constable's truncheon.

1941

668

A nymphomaniacal nurse
With a curse that was worse than perverse
 Stuck a rotary drill
 Up her twat, for a thrill –
And they carted her off in a hearse.

1939*

669

Peter, first Duke of Orange
Was limited to a miserable four-inch,
 But technique in a keyhole
 Developed his P-hole
'Til at last it got caught in the door-hinge.

1946

670

The young things who frequent picture-palaces
Have no use for this psycho-analysis.
   And although Doctor Freud
   Is distinctly annoyed
They cling to their old-fashioned fallacies.

1927*

671

There was a young fellow named Perkin
Who always was jerkin' his gherkin.
   His wife said, 'Now, Perkin,
   Stop jerkin' your gherkin;
You're shirkin' your ferkin' – you bastard!'

1938–1944A

672

There was a young girl from Peru
Who badly wanted a screw.
   She tried a broom-handle
   And the end of a candle,
But threw them away for a Jew.

1946A

673

There was a young man named Pete
Who was a bit indiscreet.
   He pulled on his dong
   Till it grew very long
And actually dragged in the street.

1939A

674

A eunuch who came from Port Said
Had a jolly good time in bed,
   Nor could any sultana
   Detect from his manner
That he used a banana instead.

1947B

675

Quoth the coroner's jury in Preston,
'The verdict is rectal congestion.'
    They found an eight-ball
    On a shoemaker's awl
Halfway up the major's intestine.

1942A

676

When Paul the Apostle lay prostrate,
And leisurely prodded his prostate,
    With pride parabolic
    His most apostolic
Appendage became an apostate.

1947

677

There was a young lady named Psyche
In bed with a fellow named Ike.
    Said he, 'Now don't worry,
    Or hurry or flurry,
But that ain't my prick – it's a spike.'

1941

678

There was a young man from Racine
Who invented a fucking machine.
    Concave or convex
    It would fit either sex,
With attachments for those in between.

1927–1938

679

And was perfectly simple to clean.
With a drip-pot to catch all the cream.
And jerked itself off in between.
The God-damndest thing ever seen.
And guaranteed used by the Queen.

1928–1950

680

There was a young man from Aberdeen
Who invented a jerking machine.
On the twenty-fifth stroke
The God damn thing broke
And beat his balls to a cream.

1950

681

There was a young lady named Rackstraw,
Titillated herself with a hack-saw.
As a result of this action
She no longer has traction,
And a penis feels just like a jackstraw.

1945–1952

682

There was a young girl named Miss Randall
Who thought it beneath her to handle
A young fellow's pole,
So instead, her hot hole
She contented by means of a candle.

1947

683

There was an Archbishop of Rheims
Who played with himself in his dreams.
On his night-shirt in front
He painted a cunt,
Which made his spend gush forth in streams.

1879

684

A cardinal living in Rome
Had a Renaissance bath in his home.
He could gaze at the nudes
As he worked up his moods
In emulsions of semen and foam.

1942A

685   HYDRAULIC INTERLUDE

There was a young lady named Rose
Who'd occasionally straddle a hose,
   And parade about, squirting
   And spouting and spurting,
Pretending she pissed like her beaux.

She was seen by her cousin named Anne,
Who improved the original plan.
   Said she, 'My dear Rose,
   In this lowly old hose
Are all the best parts of a man.'

So, avoiding the crude and sadistic,
She frigged in a manner artistic:
   At the height of her pleasure
   She turned up the pressure,
And cried, 'Ain't it grand and realistic!'

They soon told the Duchess of Fyfe,
And her crony, the alderman's wife;
   And they found it so pleasing,
   And tickling and teasing
That they washed men right out of their life.

It was tried by the great Mrs. Biddle,
And she said to her husband, 'Go fiddle!
   Here's double the fun,
   And you get three in one –
A ducking, a douche, and a diddle.'

It was tried by the dancer, Di Basle,
Whose cunt was just made for a nozzle.
  She said, 'I admit
  It's an elegant fit,
But of course it won't do for the arse 'ole.'

It was tried by the Duchess of Porter,
And passed on by her to her daughter,
  Who said, 'With a leman
  You're fearful of semen,
But a fuck's as effective with water.'

Thus writes Lady Vanderbilt-Horsett,
Who invented the Lonely-Maid Corset:
  'I thought all vicarious
  Fucking precarious.
I was wrong. It's a whiz. I endorse it.'

Soon in Paris, on the Boulevard Salique,
You could purchase (*complet avec talic,*
  Pour soixante francs cinq)
  A short hose and a tank,
And they called it *Le Fuckeur Hydraulique.*
                                    1938–1941

694.

There was a young lady named Rose,
With erogenous zones in her toes.
  She remained onanistic
  Till a foot-fetichistic
Young man became one of her beaux.
                                    1941*–1946в

695

There once was a eunuch of Roylem,
Took two eggs to the cook and said, 'Boil 'em.
   I'll sling 'em beneath
   My inadequate sheath,
And slip into the harem and foil 'em.'

1947B

696

There was a young fellow named Rule
Who went to a library school.
   As he fingered the index
   His thoughts ran to sex,
And his blood all ran to his tool.

1942

697

There was a young fellow named Rummy
Who delighted in whipping his dummy.
   He played pocket pool
   With his happy old tool
Till his shorts and his pants were all comey.

1942

698

There was a young man of St. Paul's
Possessed the most useless of balls:
   Till at last, at the Strand,
   He managed a stand,
And tossed himself off in the stalls.

1879

699

There's a pretty young lady named Sark,
Afraid to get laid in the dark,
   But she's often manhandled
   By the light of a candle
In the bushes of Gramercy Park.

1946A

700

There was a young man of Savannah,
Met his end in a curious manner.
  He diddled a hole
  In a telegraph pole
And electrified his banana.

                                1941

701

Cried her partner, 'My dear Lady Schmoosing,
While I'll own that stinkfinger's amusing,
  Still, this constant delay
  Tends to hold up the play,
And this goom on the deck's most confusing.'
                                1945

702

Girls give Jim's stiff penis a spasm
Whenever he sees 'em or has 'em.
  He likes them so well
  He needs only to smell
Them, to have a spontaneous orgasm.

                                1942

703

There was a young man of high station
Attached to the Chinese Legation.
  He liked to be fucked,
  And adored being sucked,
But he revelled in pure masturbation.
                              1879–1947B

704

A milkmaid there was, with a stutter,
Who was lonely and wanted a futter.
  She had nowhere to turn,
  So she diddled a churn,
And managed to come with the butter.

                                1941

705

A girl by the green Susquehanna
Said she would do it mañana,
   But her lover got sore
   And sailed off to Ladore . . .
And now she must use a banana.

1942A

706

There was a young genius in Texas
Who could flex his own solar plexus.
   It made his ding bounce,
   And he caught every ounce
Of his magical spraying of sexus.

1952

707

A decayed, witty old frump of Thrace
Substituted rubber in her personal place.
   She developed the trick,
   When you pulled out your prick,
Of snapping the guck in your face.

1943

708

There was a young lady of Thyme
Who swore she'd hold out for all time.
   So she stifled the crave
   For a cock in her nave,
And insisted a candle was fine.

1946A

709

A virgin felt urged in Toulouse
Till she thought she would try self-abuse.
   In search of a hard on
   She ran out in the garden,
And was had by a statue of Zeus.

1942A

710

Under the spreading chestnut tree
The village smith he sat,
   Amusing himself
   By abusing himself
And catching the load in his hat.

                     1941

711

There was a young man from Vancouver
Whose existence had lost its prime mover.
   But its loss he supplied
   With a piece of bull's hide,
Two pears, and the bag from the Hoover.

                     1941

712

There was a young fellow named Veach
Who fell fast asleep on the beach.
   His dreams of nude women
   Had his proud organ brimming
And squirting on all within reach.

                 1947ʙ

713

A widow whose singular vice
Was to keep her late husband on ice
   Said, 'It's been hard since I lost him –
   I'll *never* defrost him!
Cold comfort, but cheap at the price.'

                 1947ʙ

714

Don't dip your wick in a Wac,
Don't ride the breast of a Wave,
   Just sit in the sand
   And do it by hand,
And buy bonds with the money you save.

                 1948

715

There was a young man named Walljasper
Who invented a furlined ballclasper.
  A half turn to the right
  Would bring squeals of delight
To the most sterile, im*p*otent whoremaster.

1947B

716

There was a young man from Winsocket
Who put a girl's hand in his pocket.
  Her delicate touch
  Thrilled his pecker so much,
It shot off in the air like a rocket.

1942–1952

717

There was a young fellow from Yale
Whose face was exceedingly pale.
  He spent his vacation
  In self-masturbation
Because of the high price of tail.

1927–1941

IX CHAMBER OF HORRORS

718

A plump English prof. from Atlanta
Was bloated with bawdy, bold banter.
   He'd sit on his ass
   And let fly his gas
Whenever he sniffed a decanter.

1938

719

There once was a gangster named Brown,
The wiliest bastard in town.
   He was caught by the G-men
   Shooting his semen
Where the cops would all slip and fall down.

1938

720

There was a cute quirp from Calcutta
Who was fond of churning love-butta,
   One night she was heard mutta
   That her quim was a-flutta
For the thing she called 'Utterly-Utta!'

1943

721

An unfortunate fellow named Chase
Had an ass that was not quite in place,
   And he showed indignation
   When an investigation
Showed that some people shit through their face.

1941

722

A young man from famed Chittagong
Worked hard at the stool and worked long.
    He felt a hard mass
    Obstructing his ass,
Then shit and cried, 'I shit a gong!'

1942

723

There was a stout lady of Cuttack
Posteriorly pecked by a wild duck
    Who pursued her for miles
    And continued his wiles
Till he completely demolished her buttock.

1943*

724

It was on the 7th of December
That Franklin D. took out his member.
    He said, like the bard,
    'It will be long and very hard,
Pearl Harbor has given me something to
    remember.'   1942

725

There was a young fellow from Eno
Who said to his girl, 'Now, old Beano,
    Lift your skirt up in front,
    And enlarge your old cunt,
For the size of this organ is keen-o.'

1927

726

A maiden who dwells in Galena
Has bubbies of graceful demeanor,
    And whenever she preens
    These astounding poitrines,
She insists upon Simoniz Kleener.

1938

727

It's a helluva fix that we're in
When the geographical spread of the urge to sin
   Causes juvenile delinquency
   With increasing frequency
By the Army, the Navy, and Errol Flynn.

1947B

728

To Italy went Sinclair Lewis
Documenting the life led by loose
   American drunks,
   But he unpacked his trunks
'Cause Florence slipped him a goose.

1948A

729

There was a young fellow named Louvies
Who tickled his girl in the boovies,
   And as she contorted,
   He looked down and snorted,
'My prick wants to get in your movies!'

1927

730

A person of most any nation
If afflicted with bad constipation,
   Can shove a cuirass
   Up the crack of his ass,
But it isn't a pleasing sensation.

1941

731

I got this from the fellow what own it:
He declared that he boasted one mo' nut
   Than most people sport,
   But was terribly short
In the part you might stick through a doughnut.

1948A

732

Said my wife as she stood on a rostrum,
'I don't mind if I don't have colostrum,
 But I'll take an option
 If your child's for adoption –
Though I cannot bear kids, I can foster 'em.'

         1951

733

There was a young man in Schenectady,
And he found it quite hard to erect, said he,
 Till he took an injection
 For deficient erection,
Which in just the desired way effected he!

        1942–1952

734

There was a young student of Skat, ah me!
Who said, 'What have these wenches got o' me?
 I have lost father's knees,
 Likewise my pancreas,
And I fear I shall die of phlebotomy.'

         1938

735

An untutored Southwestern solon
Couldn't tell his behind from a hole in
 That good Texas ground
 Till the day that he found
That oil wouldn't come out of his colon.

         1948A

736

A hopeful young lady of Sukker Barrage
Possessed a big swelling she hoped would assuage.
 On her way to the train,
 She was caught in the rain –
Oh, what a sad tale of hopeless Miss Carriage!

         1943*

737

A horrid old lady of Summit,
Every time she got laid had to vomit,
   And although she would groan
   When her man got a bone,
'Give it here,' she would say, 'and I'll gum it.'
                       1952

738

There was a young girl from Vistula
To whom a friend said, 'Jeff has kissed you, la!'
   Said she, 'Yes, by God!
   But my arse he can't sod,
Because I am troubled with fistula.'
                       1879

739

There was a young man from Wanamee
Well schooled in the technique of sodomy.
   He buggered with glee
   An old man in a tree,
And remarked with a shrug, 'Won't you pardon me?'
                       1946B

740

Said a platinum blonde from Warsaw,
As she looked at herself in the raw,
   ' 'Neath my umbilicus
   (And as like Mike as Ike is)
There's a picture of George Bernard Shaw.'
                       1941

X ADDENDA

741   EXCREMENT

There's always some one around
Who'd object if I rifted with sound.
   But out in the park,
   At least after dark,
I can make the welkin resound.

1951

742

There was a young student of art
Who made a strange anatomical chart:
   In place of the chest
   A grease spot on the vest,
And in place of the asshole a fart.

1944

743

There was an old maid from Bruton
Who had the bad habit of pootin'.
   Her sphincter was weak,
   Her wind she couldn't keep –
This tootin' old spinster from Bruton.

1951

744

Said a snuff-taking Turk, 'Why, with ease
I can stifle the noisiest sneeze.'
   But at prayers one day
   His ass-hole gave way,
And the shit filled his drawers to the knees.

1952

745

A flatulent nun of Hawaii
One Easter eve supped on papaya,
   Then honored the Passover
   By turning her ass over
And obliging with Handel's Messiah.

1944

746

There was a young man from Montmartre
Who was famed far and wide for his fart.
   When they said, 'What a noise!'
   He replied with great poise,
'When I fart, sir, I fart from the heart.'

1945

747

There was a young man named O'Malley
Who was fucking his gal in the alley,
   When right at the start
   She let a small fart,
Said O'Malley to Sally, 'Now r'ally!'

1951

748

A stingy old man of St. Giles
Saved his shillings with miserly wiles.
   Just to save a few bob
   He would wipe with a cob,
And that way he got piles and piles!

1941

749

Lord Randall, on top of his tart,
Let a horrible, fizzling fart.
   Said the tart, 'Now, m'lord,
   I'm taking your word
You did not follow through on the spot.'

1952

750   ZOOPHILY

There once was a Bactrian camel
Who was bound by no fetter or trammel.
  When he tried to make hay
  In his Bactrian way,
His wife said, 'Make me; I'm a mammal.'

               1943

751

There was a young girl from Decatur
Who was fucked by an old alligator.
  No one ever knew
  How she relished that screw,
For after he fucked her, he ate her.

               1944

752

A zoologist's daughter in Ewing
Gave birth to a bottle of bluing.
  Her father said, 'Flo,
  What I want to know
Isn't *whether*, but *what* you've been screwing.'

When the girl replied, quick as a wink,
'My child isn't bluing, it's ink,'
  The professor said, 'Ah!
  Then, no doubt, its papa
Is the squid that I keep in the sink.'

               1944

754

There was a young person of Jaipur
Who fell madly in love with a viper.
  With screams of delight
  He'd retire each night
With the viper concealed in his diaper.

               1944

755

A disgusting young man named McGill
Made his neighbors exceedingly ill
When they learned of his habits
Involving white rabbits
And a bird with a flexible bill.

1944

756

There was an old maid in Nantucket,
Had an asshole as big as a bucket.
While bent over the oven,
A-dreamin' of lovin',
Her goat seized the moment to fuck it.

1952

757

There was a young man who preferred
Having sex with some kind of a bird.
The rarer the species,
And the fuller of feces,
The better – that guy really loved turd.

1951–1952

758

There once was a fellow named Siegel
Who attempted to bugger a beagle,
But the mettlesome bitch
Turned and said with a twitch,
'It's fun, but you know it's illegal.'

1943

759

There was a young fellow named Spratt
Who was terribly sassy and fat.
He sat amusing himself
By abusing himself,
While his trained leopard licked at his pratt.

1944

760

On the plains of north-central Tibet
They've thought of the strangest thing yet:
   On the ass of a camel
   They pour blue enamel,
And bugger the beast while it's wet.

1944

761

A milkmaid of Warnesby Fair
Was an expert at riding bulls bare.
   Oh how the bulls gallop
   To give that dear trollop
A bounce on the sweet derry-air.

1945

762

In the quaint English village of Worcester
Lived a little red hen and a rooster.
   A coquettish glance
   She acquired in France
Gave him ants in his pants, and he goosed her.

1944

763

Said an old-fashioned god named Anubis,
'I know about pubes and boobies,
   But I've no impression
   About the Eustachian,
Or where the Fallopian tube is.'

1952

764

There once was a sensitive bride
Who ran when the groom she espied.
   When she looked at his swiver
   They had to revive her,
But when he got it well in, she just sighed.

1952

765

Ein lustiger Geck namens Franz,
Er zerrte einmal seinen Schwanz.
    Um sein männliches Glied
    Verband er ein Ried,
Nun also ficken er kanns.

1952

766

Said the horrible whore of Lahore
While ape-fucking against a door,
    'This orang-utang
    Is better than bhang –
The penis of man is quite a bore.'

1918*–1952

767

There once was a young man named Lanny
The size of whose prick was uncanny.
    His wife, the poor dear,
    Took it into her ear,
And it came out the hole in her fanny.

1952

768

Two pretty young twins named Mahony
Once tickled a horse's baloney.
    With a spurt and a splash
    They fell with a crash,
And no one knew which had the Toni.

1952

769

There was a young lady of Norway
Who hung by her heels in a doorway.
    She said to her beau,
    'Look at me, Joe,
I think I've discovered one more way.'

1952

770

There was a young girl from Odessa,
A rather unblushing transgressor.
   When sent to the priest
   The lewd little beast
Began to undress her confessor.

1952

771

A scandal involving an oyster
Sent the Countess of Clewes to a cloister.
   She preferred it in bed
   To the count, so she said,
Being longer, and stronger, and moister.

1952

772

There was a young man from Peru
Whose lineage was noble all through.
   Now this isn't crud
   For not only his blood
But even his semen was blue.

1952

773

A lecherous priest from Peru
Fucked the deacon's wife in a pew.
   'I'll admit I'm not pious,'
   He said, 'I've a bias –
I think it diviner to screw.'

1952

774

Cleopatra, while helping to pump,
Ground out such a furious bump
   That Antony's dick
   Snapped off like a stick,
And left him to pump with the stump.

1952

775

A certain young lady named Rowell
Had a musical vent to her bowel.
   With a good plate of beans
   Tucked under her jeans
She could play To a Wild Rose by MacDowell.

1947B

776

The parish commission at Roylette
Bought their vicar a pristine new toilet.
   But he still voids his bowels
   On a heap of old towels,
He's so very reluctant to soil it.

1949

777

There was a young man named Royal
Whose ambition was to be a *moyhel*.
   He worked and he toiled
   But was finally foiled
When he tried it out on a goil.

1943*

778

There was a young lady named Shriver
Who was screwed in the ass by the driver,
   And when she complained
   He said, 'Sorry you were pained,'
And gave her a fiver to bribe her.

1952

779

A muscular Turk of Stamboul
Tried to screw a recalcitrant mule.
   He climbed on a haystack
   Overlooking a racetrack,
And dived in all covered with drool.

1952

780

There once was an artist named Thayer
Who was really a cubist for fair.
   He looked all his life
   To find him a wife
Possessed of a cunt that was square.

1952

781

A frugal young fellow named Wise
Gets the most from the dead whores he buys.
   After sporting a while
   As a gay necrophile,
For dessert he has maggot surprise.

1952

782

A certain professor named Yarrow
Had trouble seducing a sparrow.
   When he'd given up hopin'
   He pried her jaws open,
And filled up her bill with his marrow.

1952

783   CHAMBER OF HORRORS

A bishop there was of Pyongyang
Who offered an actress his dong.
   She cried, ' 'Pon my Seoul
   I have a huge hole,
But your thing's just comme-ci Kumsong.'

1952

784

There was a young man from Saskatchewan
Whose pecker was truly gargantuan.
   It was good for large whores
   And small dinosaurs,
And sufficiently rough to scratch a match upon.

1952

NOTE

The following limerick sequences, and ballads more or less in the limerick form, are included in Volume One:

NOTES AND VARIANTS

NOT-QUITE-LIMERICKS: Here's To It, 103; It's Only Human Nature, 104; Iowa, 157; Tom, Tom, the Piper's Son, 188; Son's-a-Bitches, 201; Ten-Ten-Tennessee, 461; The Spanish Nobilio, 465; I Lost My Arm, 483; Screwy Dick, 508; The Village Smith, 710; Don't Dip Your Wick, 714.

STRANGE INTERCOURSE

1. Il y avait un jeune homme de Dijon,
   Qui n'avait que peu de religion.
     Il dit, 'Quant à moi,
     Je m'encule tous les trois –
   Le Père, et le Fils, et le Pigeon.'   [1928–1939A

2. Spanish-speaking peoples have a fine sacrilegious style of oath and invective, swearing, for instance, 'By the twenty-four testicles of the twelve Apostles of Christ!' 'By the ass-hole of God!' or 'By the blessed cunt of the Virgin Mary, which I would have fucked if I had had the time!' For another Spanish limerick, see 769 in Vol. II.

4. On the movie-actress Mary Astor, whose sex-diary ('Twenty minutes – I don't know how he does it!') was published in the New York tabloids during her divorce in the 1930s.

5. On Auden and Isherwood, minor British poets of the period.

7. Parodied in Limerick 904 in Vol. II.

9.   His twenty inch peter
     (A triple repeater)
     Would come like the Biblical Flood!   [1948

10. Note the obscene public interest in the sex life of famous
    cripples: the man in the iron lung, President Franklin D.
    Roosevelt (Note 32), etc.

12.   Said the king, as he came,
      To this cow-cunted dame: [1941

    In his *Quaderni d'anatomia*, folio 7 recto, note 5, Leonardo
    da Vinci gives a burlesque demonstration that the cunt of a
    woman is proportionately three times as large as that of a
    cow. Compare the burlesque discussions of the 'Intronati' in
    Antonio Vignale's *La Cazzaria* (1530), MS. translation by
    Samuel Putnam, who discusses the work in *Encyclopaedia
    Sexualis* (N.Y., 1936), pp. 491–2.

14.   But 'tweren't the Almighty
      That lifted her nightie   [1941

      Though she had been worked over
      'Twas not by Jehovah,
    But a man with a fifteen-inch rod.   [1949

18. COAST (Boast). Variant: 'Said the wan ectoplasm,' heighten-
    ing the note of wistful sadness. Compare Limerick 140, and
    Philippe Quinault's *The Amorous Fantasme* (English transla-
    tion, 1661).

      A terrible spasm
      Passed over her chasm
    While the fellow was browning his toast.   [1948

21.   Not a murmur was heard,
      Not a sound, not a word   [1943A

23. Limerick version of an incest theme well-known in folk tales,
    often with the revenge element of transmitting venereal
    disease to a male enemy by these (repressed homosexual)
    means.

26. Nil desperandum. Compare Limerick 373.

27. This is of course the opening of Sterne's *Tristram Shandy*
    (1760). Much material exists on the clock as Conscience
    (Freud, *Collected Papers*, 2: 158–9; and A. M. Meerloo, in
    Psychiatric Quarterly, 1948–50) and on Father Time as
    Kronos the castrator. Improved:

    > He buggered the clock
    > With the end of his cock,
    > And wound up his wife with the key.   [1946A

    > He cut off his cock
    > In winding the clock,
    > So he fucked his wife with the key.   [1939A

28. Apocryphal whore's boast (Pa. 1940): 'I can suck you off,
    jerk you off, or take out my glass eye and wink you off.'
    Hirschfeld (1914) quotes from Rohleder, 'coitus in cavitatem
    oculi extracti.'

29. Three ingenious young siblings called Biddle
    Indulged in a three-cornered diddle.
    > Though those on each side
    > Were well satisfied,
    All fought for dual joys in the middle.   [1942

    Punch-line of a well-known joke, becoming a catch-phrase:
    'Lucky Julius (*or* Pierre), always in the middle!' The name
    has been used alone, as a recondite bawdry, in *Time* and in
    Al Capp's 'Li'l Abner.'

37. Robert Ripley, *Believe It Or Not* (1929), p. 169: 'The Em-
    press Marie Louise [Napoleon's second wife] could fold her
    ears at will – and also turn them inside out!' The under side
    of the upper crust. Compare Limericks 172, 228 and 782 in
    Vol. II.

38. Who lost it one night in Peoria.
    > Then she lost some more cherries
    > At Pierre's and at Sherry's,
    But most at the Waldorf-Astoria.   [1943B

Song: 'She Had To Go and Lose It At the Astor' (music by 'John Doe & Joe Doaques', 1939).

43. A reporter named Archibald Symes
    Lured girls on to infamous crimes.
        'I give them,' he'd boast,
        'Two Globes and a Post,
    And God knows how many Times.'   [1942

    This joke, on how many newspapers of these names a news-
    girl can hold between her legs, illustrated in *Broadway
    Brevities* (10 October 1932).

44. HILDA (Brunnhilde, Ilder). See Limerick 493.

46. Parodying a famous original by Cosmo Monkhouse.

47.   To Betty-Jane Kuntz
       Who took three men at once –   [1941

    This heroine appears under the name Lyde (as noted in *Index
    Limericus*) in an epigram in the Greek Anthology, V. 49,
    translated into Latin thus:

    Lyde, quae tribus viris eadem celeritate inservit, Huic supra
    ventrem, illi subter, alii a postico. Admitto, inquit, paedi-
    conem, mulierosum, irrumatorem. Si festinas, etiam si cum
    duobus ingressus sis, ne te cohibeas.

    Compare Martial IX. 32, also Limerick 498, and the recent
    Purim poem (1947) beginning:

        Oh, Esther was a three-way queen,
        She wasn't very moral.
        She took the king in every way –
        Vaginal, anal, oral.

49. One of the most famous limericks, with gag variant: 'And
    instead of coming he sneezed, or shit, or jacked off' (1938*).

50. KILDARE (Astaire, BelAir, Bulgair, Carstair, Clair, Eau
    Claire, Klare, MacNair, Montclair, nowhere). Compare the

geographical variants of Limerick 202, and, with the version below, the mathematical variants of Limerick 169. The number of the crucial stroke varies from the twenty-first in *Immortalia* (1927) to the sixty-third in Douglas (1928) as below:

> Who was having a girl in a chair.
>> At the sixty-third stroke
>> The furniture broke,
> And his rifle went off in the air.   [1928

51. As every schoolboy knows, this is an abbreviation of the Welsh name Llanfairpwllgwyngyllgogerychwyrndrobwyll-tysiliogogogoch, on which Langford Reed, *The Complete Limerick Book* (2 ed., 1926), p. 189*, asks for a 'hero to venture an example'.

52. Stacked-chairs position. Compare Variant 47.

55. Compare: 'Wife: an attachment you screw on the bed to get the housework done.'

64. Actually Young had only 21 wives. His reputation as a man of parts may not, however, have been entirely without foundation. At his birthplace in Whitingham, Vermont, a simple marker records: 'Brigham Young, born on this spot 1801, a man of much courage and superb equipment.'

66.   And, being quite lewd
>> She asked to be screwed
> In the ass by her friend John O'Rourke.   [1946A

69.   And he hadn't much patience
>> With the girl's objurgations.   [1941

71. PENZANCE (France). The original of both theme and rhyme is Limerick 90 (see Vol. II) sixty years before. The texts vary greatly, one version making it a train, not a bus, and ending: 'The engineer shit (*not* shot) in his pants.'

72. 'Perhaps the colloquial comparative, "hotter than a Persian fuck," should be changed to "longer . . ." '
– *Lapses in Limerick* (1938).

74. Possibly the lunar climate. See Limerick 59.

75. Generally said to refer to Mrs. Wallis Warfield Simpson, 'who fucked the King of England out of the throne' (1936).

> When she said to her swain,
> 'Let's do it again!'   [1941

> Said the driver, 'Encore!'
> But the man just got sore   [1949

There was a young lady named Ransom
Who was ravished three times in a cab.
> When she cried out for more,
> Came a voice from beneath:
'Lady, my name is Sanders, not Sandow.'   [1944

80. On newspaper correspondent Walter Duranty's *I Write As I Please* (1935).

82. This ugly autobiographical fantasy appears only in Clement Wood's *The Facts of Life in Limericks* (1943). The theme is repeated, in a slightly glozed form, in a new story added to the reprint of his collection of short stories, *Flesh*, before his death.

84. SPAIN (Lorraine, Steubén). Variants: 'Who was raped by an ape on a train' (1944), 'Who delighted to pee in the rain' (1952); but the text form has the real Gothic flavor.

86. 'The last line should be read with leering envy.' – *Index Limericus* (1943). Variant:

There was a young fellow of Sydney
Who with women and wine ruined his kidney.
> He screwed and he boozed,
> And his innards all oozed,
But he had a good time of it, didn' he ?   [1941

87. TIBET (Turkish cadet). Wells, 1951, notes a 'religious motif' in this, suggesting a variant on a Tibetan *priest*.

    With the greatest of ease
    He could rape six Chinese   [1948A

89. There was a young man from Toledo
    Who traveled about incognito.
        The reason he did
        Was to bolster his id
    While appeasing his savage libido   [1949

91. With a cockswain or two, for good measure. [1941

93.   Till one day with a cousin
        He ripped off a dozen   [1948A

95. Omitting the Man in the Moon limericks (59 and 74) from
    the consideration, this and the preceding are the first science-
    fiction limericks.

97. Compare 'fish, fuck, faint, and fall over', *fish* referring to
    oragenitalism, *fall over* to passive pedication (N.Y., 1939),
    and the song 'Mary Lou' (in *North Atlantic Squadron*,
    Gander Bay, Newfoundland, 1944, mimeographed), ending:
    'She can ride, fart, fight, fuck, shoot the shit and drive a
    truck, That's the kind of a sonovabitch that's gonna marry
    me.'

99. Y.T.: Young Thing. Variant: 'There was a young twirp of
    Ave. B.' (1943B).

103. Toast (by a Lady): 'In with it, and out with it, and God work
     his will with it.' – *The Pearl*, no. 16 (October 1880).

        Here's to it and from it
        And to it again.
        May the man who got to it
        And then didn't do it,
        May he never get to it
        To do it again.   [N.Y., 1939

104. To line a pretty girl against the wall,
        To stick your continuation
        In her communication –
     It's human nature, that's all.   [1943

105. 'They A' Do't.' From *The Pearl*, no. 8 (February 1880), intruded in Part IV of 'Lady Pokingham, or They All Do It', with note: 'to the tune of "A man's a man for a' that" '. The origin of this Scottish song is a mystery. It does not appear in the first edition of Robert Burns' *Merry Muses of Caledonia* (Dumfries, *c*. 1800), but is included by Duncan M'Naught (*Merry Muses*, ed. 1911, Introduction) in a list of additions first published in the edition 'Dublin: Printed for the Booksellers, 1832', which has not been available for collation. The asterisked line in the second verse is a forgery by the present editor to fill an apparent lacuna in the text.

EXCREMENT

117. Castoria: a patent laxative for babies.

124.   There's an end to his wit
         'Twas a handful of shit   [1948A

125. Cleaned up couplet in *Peter Pauper's Limerick Book* (ed. 1942), p. 24: 'She didn't dare bend, For fear she'd offend.' LaBarre (1939), p. 209 erroneously notes: 'A fat lady of Bryde was afraid to re-tie her shoe-laces for fear of incontinence of feces [!]'

126. Variant conclusion: 'It's longer than marster's – and hairier!' (1945), with which compare a similar dénouement to a game of 'Bride's Buff' in the kitchen, in *The Last of the Bleshughs* 'by the Marquis de Fartanoys' [Roy McCardell; New York, *c*. 1928], reprinted, with erotic illustrations added, from *Secret Memoirs* (1928), v. 2: pp. 481–99. McCardell's erotic work includes 'The Quimbo Lexicon', in *Observations of An Old Man in Love* ('Philadelphia', 1929), pretendedly an interlude from Frank Harris' *Life and Loves* (see Limerick 888 in Vol. II).

128. Compare 'Calcutta Curio', Limerick 345 in Vol. II.

129. Punning on the World War II phrase, 'shit for the birds', meaning lies, buncombe.

132. On the need to 'learn, read, or accomplish other tasks during defaecation', see Karl Abraham, *Selected Papers* (1927), International Psycho-Analytical Library, v. 13: p. 385, 'Contributions to the Theory of the Anal Character.'

135. CHISELHURST (Hazelhurst, Thistlehurst). Better-rhyming, more castratory, and probably the original conclusion:

    And before he remembered, his pizzle burst.   [1947

    The effect of whistling on the genitals in easing urination, is noted at least as far back as the original *Mother Goose's Melody* (intra 1768–80) ed. 1791, p. 48, the editor – apparently Oliver Goldsmith, a physician as well as a writer – noting, concerning the famous non-sequitur song, 'Three children sliding on the ice': 'There is something so melancholy in this song, that it has occasioned many people to make water. It is almost as diuretic as the tune which John the coachman whistles to his horses.' – Trumpington's *Travels*. Compare Shakespeare's *Henry IV*, Part II, Act III. ii. 346.

143.   But having got there
        (S)he let out only air   [1949

145. By George Moore, as cited by Padraic Colum, in *Esquire* (March 1936), p. 62.

146. The Old Lady, alias of Ealing, will be found under Wheeling, Limerick 211.

147. 'Excusado', Spanish for toilet, and not for 'excuse me' or similar; therefore the occasion of many traveler's tales of embarrassing confusion.

148.   From pity and terror
        They committed the error
        Of weeping – alas! – from their arses.   [1942

149. A similar odyssey of a fly-button is used with telling effect in Norman Douglas' *South Wind* (1917). Variant: 'With the aid of a sound . . .'

150. Compare the music-hall song, 'I 'ad a banana with Lydy Diana.'

151. *Lapses in Limerick* notes, in 'And they felt even fouler than that,' an admirable avidity for empiric research. Compare Limerick 324 in Vol. II.

155. In other words: a shit brickhouse.

156. Compare Limerick 360 in Vol. II.

157. Schweinickle (1928), p. 61, as a reply by the Congressman from Iowa to the following toast by the Congressman from Maine:

> 'Here's to the American Eagle,
> That beautiful bird of prey:
> He flies from Maine to Mexico,
> And he shits on Iowa.'

An encounter almost as desperate is recorded in 'The Rival Toasts', in *The Pearl*, no. 1 (July 1879) – just preceding the first batch of limericks – in which 'Captain Balls . . . of the Yankee frigate' offers as a toast, on an English man o' war: 'Here's to the glorious American flag: Stars to enlighten all nations, and Stripes to flog them.' To which Jack, 'the old ship's steward' on the Englishman, egged on by his captain, offers the reply: 'Then here's to the ramping, roaring, British Lion, who shits on the stars, and wipes his arse on the stripes.'

158. Langford Reed, *The Complete Limerick Book* (1925), p. 210, the only off-color specimen Reed allows himself – possibly out of sheer misunderstanding.

161. Douglas notes briefly, 'As to the victim being now in Heaven – we must take our poet's word for that. I think, unless they have fished him out, he will be found where he was.'

163. On *Gone With the Wind* – from Dowson's *Cynara* – popularized by the novel (1936) by the Georgian writer, Margaret Mitchell.

164. The plot essentials of a party-record called 'The Farting Contest' (Canada, *c*. 1940) with superlative sound effects and the same last line.

166. MACHIAS (Matthias, Mount Tamalpais, Tobias).
    They were fixed with a loop
    Through which she could poop   [1946A

    With a slit in the middle
    Through which she could piddle   [1940*

168. Compare Limerick 134.

169. Douglas notes that the soprano is the part beginning, 'Send her victorious . . .' Compare, in 'The Star-Spangled Banner', the equally impossible passage for soprano beginning 'Whose broad stripes and bright stars . . .' On musical farting generally, see Limerick 189.

172. Ciano: a minor Fascist functionary, married to Mussolini's daughter, Edda, and executed by his father-in-law in 1944.

174.   And sent it to Spain
    With a note to explain
    That it came from his grandmother's arsell.   [1928

    Received a remarkable parcel:
    In a box with three locks
    Were two cocks with the pox,
    And a quim, and the brim of an arsehole.   [1941

    In it, I've heard,
    Was a transparent turd   [1952

Compare: *a blivet*: two pounds of shit in a one-pound bag (thrown out an upper-storey window to splatter on the pave when one has no toilet – also called 'sending the air-mail'), *a trivet*: a pound of shit stuffed in the toe of an old sock, and used as a blackjack; and *a rivet*: a mashed-potato turd stuffed down a sink (1952).

178.   She woke with a start
        And let a loud fart,
     Which was followed by luncheon and dinner.   [1928

Douglas notes the strict logic of the excretion (p. 71), with
which compare 'To the Critics and Poets', in *The New Boghouse Miscellany, or A Companion for the Close-stool* (1761)
pp. 207–15:

     There was a jovial butcher,
     He liv'd at Northern-fall-gate,
        He kept a stall
        At Leadenhall,
     And got drunk at the boy at Aldgate.

     He ran down Hounsditch reeling,
     At Bedlam he was frighted,
        He in Moorfields
        Besh-t his heels
     And at Hoxton he was wiped.

The anonymous critic noting (p. 214) how in the second
verse 'The geography of the places where the action happened, is strictly observed . . .' Although the limerick form
can be traced to 'Tom o' Bedlam's Song' (*c.* 1610) and
'Sumer is icumen in' (*c.* 1300); this example, 'To the Critics'
(which may be reprinted from Newbery's magazine *The Midwife, c.* 1750), is the earliest 'geographical' limerick as yet
discovered, and has certainly enough place-names, false
rhymes, and even a 'There was . . .' to satisfy any historian.

180–81. First Egyptologist (on finding a pile of fresh shit in the
     unopened tomb): 'Dr. Carter, do you think possibly a cat
     crept into the crypt and crapped and crept out again?'
     Second Egyptologist: 'No, I think it was the pup popped into
     the pit and pooped and then popped out.'

182. Variant: 'With a roar like a double bassoon' (1941). The
     bassoon is the typical farting instrument of the orchestra,
     consciously so used in Richard Strauss' 'Tyl Eulenspiegel' to

show Tyl's fright at the scaffold. Lady: 'Does the bassoonist really make that noise with his mouth?' Conductor: 'I hope so.' (Dr. Paul Englisch, *Das skatologische Element in Literatur*, 1928, p. 57.)

186. And at night piss all over the hall. [1943

188. Quoted by Morse (1948, p. 9, from *The Eternal Eve* [Cleveland?] 1941, p. 166.

189.   He could fart anything
       From God Save the King   [1938
       (From Stravinsky to swing)   [1952

As observed by *Index Limericus*, 'St. Augustine, in his *De Civitate Dei* (d. 430), refers to an individual possessed of this talent.' The themes of music and farting (Notes 164, 182) are perhaps inseparable. Sándor Ferenczi, 'On Obscene Words', in his *Contributions to Psycho-analysis* (Boston, 1916), p. 143, notes, concerning a homosexual flatophile: 'The infantile interest for the sounds accompanying the emission of intestinal gas was not without influence on his choice of profession. He became a musician.' See Limericks 139 (Vol. II) (variant: '. . . an accordion-pleated vagina; With the aid of a fart, She could render in part'), 116, 135, 150, 159 (on the present rhymes), 212, and Douglas' note, p. 40, on 169, the *vox humana* and 'pétophone.' See also 775.

201. Quoted by William Martin Camp, *Retreat, Hell!* (1943), p. 52, with note: 'It was a little ditty we made up in Shanghai,' apparently on the pattern of the non-limerick song, 'The Pioneers', (also varied as 'The Engineers'):

The pioneers have hairy ears
    They piss through leather britches;
They wipe their ass on broken glass,
    Those hardy sons-of-bitches! . . .   [1927

202. A masochistic young man of Split
     Ate his peaches complete with the pit.

'Twas not for the stone,
  He claimed, but alone
For the smart that remained when he shit.

[1944–1952

204. Douglas, p. 71, notes the almost complete lack of polysyll-
     ables. Variant: 'Which, I think, left the honors with me'
     (1943A).

211. There was a young lady of Ealing,
       Who had such a curious feeling,
         She'd lie on her back
         And tickle her crack,
     And spend right bang up to the ceiling.   [1870

     The original of the first limerick I ever heard (*c.* 1925). Drake
     calls it 'the schoolboy limerick par excellence, crammed with
     droll errors of psychology, physiology, and anatomy' (1949).
     Variants: Darjeeling, free wheeling.

ZOOPHILY

216. 'George Archibald Bishop' [Aleister Crowley], *White Stains*
     [London] 1898, p. 109, 'With Dog and Dame':

       I yield him place: his ravening teeth
         Cling hard to her – he buries him
       Insane and furious in the sheath
         She opens for him – wide and dim
       My mouth is amorous beneath . . .

218.   Just for a whim
       He dressed up as a quim   [1928

       He made up as a tree
       Having failed to foresee
     Being pissed on by dogs, cats, and all.   [1949

219. Christina Stead, *Letty Fox: Her Luck* (N.Y., 1946), pp. 293–4, describing a party at which dirty jokes, etc. are being told by both women and men: 'The Washington miss ... said, with timid eagerness, "That's very good. Do you like limericks? We go in more for limericks in Washington".' With a variant of the present example, ending 'And leaves them alone with Mamma', and the implication that mild types like these are not 'really good'. A similar scene on the telling of dirty jokes appears in Viña Delmar's *Bad Girl* (1928), pp. 37–8; and compare Richard Waterman, 'The Role of obscenity in the folk tales of the "intellectual" stratum of our society', in *Journal of American Folklore* (April 1949), v. 62: pp. 162–5.

221. BRUNO (Buno, Guantanamo, San Bruno, Yuno). All members of the American camel family appear in variants of the last line: alpaca, guanaco, etc.

223. Douglas very correctly notes, from the *Sketches of Moral Philosophy* by Sydney Smith (d. 1845), 'We shall generally find that the triangular person has got into the square hole ... and a square person has squeezed himself into the round hole.' Compare also the Biblical injunction (*Matthew*, 5:22) that 'whosoever shall say, Thou fool, shall be in danger of hell fire'.

> Said she, 'You damned shit,
> You can't fuck a bit'   [1879

> Said the ape, 'Something's wrong
> With the shape of your prong'   [1941

> Said the ape, 'Sir, your prick
> Is too long and too thick,
> And something is wrong with the shape.' [1928

228. The fice or feist-hound (lap dog), so called from its farting habits (feist: a wet fart).

233. Collected as verse 1 only of a 'Ballad of Artificial Insemination' (N.Y., 1945A), the remainder being lost.

234. DUNDEE (Capri, McGee, Paree, Pooree). An extremely
popular limerick with many variants as to 'the result,' all
apparently intended to explain the rainbow-assed monkey.

There once was a heathen Chinee
Who briggled an ape in a tree.   [1948A

 The result of the fuck
 Was a bald-headed duck,   [1946A

Blue ass and a purple J.T. (*John Thomas*)   [1943B

There was a young man from Bombay
Who raped a baboon in the hay.
  The results were most horrid –
  All ass and no forehead,
Three balls and a purple toupée.   1942

There was a young girl of the Cape
Who had an affair with an ape.
  The result was quite 'orrid,
  All ass, and no forrid,
And one of its balls was a grape!   [1951

238. EAU CLAIRE (Kildare, Knair, McNair, St. Clair).
Made friends with a cinnamon bear,
  But the treacherous brute
  Made a pass at his fruit,
And left only buttons and hair.   [1945

240. Non-zoophilous couplet and conclusion:
  But really she burned for it,
  Squirmed for it, yearned for it,
Cried for it nightly in torrents.   [1941

241. Compare Limericks 225 and 591.

242. Variant, apparently on Miss Madeleine Slade, recipient of
Gandhi's *Bapu's Letters to Mira*, with a fine colloquial rhyme
in the couplet:

Woke up one morning, quite randy.
  He called for Miss Slade,
  Or a goat instead   [1942

Whose clothes were exceedingly scanty.
  To scratch his left ball
  Was no trouble at all –
In fact, 'twas convenient and handy.   [1951

243. Compare Limerick 422, and, with Note 234:
There once was a maid from Geneva
Who kept a giraffe to relieve her.
  The result of this fuck
  Was a four-legged duck,
Three eggs, and a spotted retriever.   [1932*–1950

244. Something of an inevitable rhyme; compare in Henry
Miller's *The Booster* (later *Delta*, November 1937), back
cover:

    Out of the gorse
  Came a homosexual horse.

Other name variants: Dorse, Morse. Two variant conclusions
referring to Robinson Jeffers' *Roan Stallion* (1925), both with
female protagonists:

  A roan stallion charged her
  And so much enlarged her
That her husband applied for divorce.   [1941

  'I used to love heifers
  Until I read Jeffers,
But now I could go for this horse!'   [1938*

258. 'I've found in the course of philanderin''   [1942*

259. Burlesque book-title: *The Wildcat's Revenge*, by Claude
Balls. (List of 185 such titles, Utah 1952.)

260. She did so becuz
    She imagined the buzz   [1943

261. Next morning at dawn
She started to spawn [1945c

When nine months had passed
She had crabs up her ass [1943b

What she conceived was a sin,
All beard and no chin [1952

With motions phenomenal
And contortions abdominal,
The turtle made Myrtle fertile. [1948

262. Said the pig with a grunt,
'Get away from my cunt –' [1944

269. So he sat on a mat
And fucked the cat [1939a

So he whipped out his carrot
And diddled a parrot
– The offspring reminds me of you! [1944a

270. Consciously borrowing the couplet of Limerick 297. Variant:
'An heir to the Portuguese crown' [1943a

277. Compare with Limerick 389 in Vol. II:
He tripped on a rug
And buggered a bug,
But the bug hardly minded at all. [1944a

279. Douglas (1928), p. 73, giving lines 1–4 only, a number of
Learic last lines have been cobbled together by various hands,
on the style of: 'And fooled (foiled?) that old man of Santander.' Limerick 280 (Toulouse) first in *Anecdota Americana*
II (1934) with the Santander couplet.

281. Boulton and Park, two homosexuals of the period, put on
trial in April 1870. A contemporary cut showing them in
women's clothes and men's is reproduced in Michael Sad-
leir's *Forlorn Sunset* (N.Y., 1946), chap. 26, pt. 2, p. 305. On
talking pigs and pig-fuckers, see Limericks 262 and 265.

291. One of ten similar 'Limericks About Children, For Children, by One who doesn't like 'em', this being the only one at all approaching the erotic element. A sample of the others, with the castratory fear – quite clear in the last line – displaced on the mother-image, as in *Hansel and Gretel* (the witch who bites the child's finger to see if he's plump enough to eat):

An old Irish witch named Maloney
Cackled, 'Chicken is terribly bony.
   But a son or a daughter
   Will make your mouth water,
   And is boneless as fresh-cut baloney.'   **[1948A**

Compare a bus-advertisement for Hebrew National Kosher delicatessen, in the Jewish sections of New York, 1952, showing an enormous knife cutting into a large bologna (flanked by olives), with the caption: 'For the SLICE of Your Life!' See also Isaac Rosenfeld, 'Adam and Eve on Delancey Street', in *Commentary* (October 1949), v. 8: pp. 385–7.

293. See Note 261.

297. 'Mayor of Southampton' (also of Southbridge), 'Bishop of Oxford' (Avery, Bavory, Chatsworth, or Worcester), Earl Lavery, of Waverly. In *Life in a Putty-knife Factory* (1943), p. 144, H. Allen Smith notes a fondness for the couplet here (obviously from Limerick 273 in Vol. II) in 'John Steinbeck [who] had two thirds of the bottle of brandy inside of him by that time ... and every few minutes he'd take another sip and cry out:

> *With lecherous howls,*
> *I deflower young owls!'*

GOURMANDS

305. In a list of fruits inserted into and eaten out of the vagina during cunnilinctus: 'strawberries or cherries (sweet, pitted cherries), or sections of an orange (a seedless orange), or

slices of apple deliciously dipped in honey', in *Oragenitalism: Pt. I. Cunnilinctus*, by 'Roger-Maxe de La Glannège', [New York], 1940, p. 38, the banana is omitted!

310. Compare Limericks 174 (this volume) and 674 (Vol. II).

311. And a bloody good substitute, too.   [1928

316. FRITZ (Biarritz, Cadiz, Fitts, Hitz, McFitz, Moritz, Ritz, St. Kitts). With this standard oral-incorporative fantasy of the nursing period, compare Limerick 566. Davis (1946), p. 41, notes the interesting repressed variant: 'Last line sometimes massacred to: ("No last line: what would you do with an acre of tits?")'. *Lapses* (1941): 'But the real thrill in titi-culture is running around barefoot over the budding bubbies.' Intended as a joke, this has been translated into merely gruesome quasi-fact in the 'Falsie-Mat', sold in New York bar-appliance shops, 1950, and composed of unseparated false breasts of foam rubber, to be used as a bath mat. See the advertisement in *Billboard* (N.Y., 7 January 1950), quoted by Albert Ellis, *The Folklore of Sex* (1951), p. 113, beginning: 'ACRES AND ACRES OF 'EM!' in clear reminiscence of this limerick.

317. The last item in *Anecdota Americana II* (1934) with the note, concerning the author: 'What a mind!' Compare Limerick 330. Variants: 'A son of a bitch by marriage' (1950), 'Whose actions, no doubt, you'll disparage' (1946B).

322. Query: 'hypercritical'? Written by a committee, and presented with apologies for the poor rhyme.

323. LEITH (Dalkeith, Galbreathe, Keith, Leaf). Compare Limerick 270 in Vol. II, a much earlier version.

326. *Index Limericus* (1946) comments: 'Couldn't he get any government relief, or OPA, or something?'

327.   When these grew humdrum
        She would suck up the scum   [1941

329.   From the bellies of birds
        (S)he squeezed little turds,
        And tickled dogs' cocks till they shot in 'em.   [1943B

331.   At formal affairs
        She'd shit on the stairs   [1952

334. From the whole tone, impossible rhyme, etc. of this apotheosis of the theme of the Jew-as-castrator, one would really expect 'blood' not 'piss' in the couplet.

337. Compare the added-foot form of Limericks 323 and 280 in Vol. II.

339. 'The poor fellow was living in typographical error. He had evidently mistaken colitis for coitus.' – *Lapses in Limerick* (1938).

341. Compare Limerick 278 in Vol. II. Depression joke (*c.* 1932): 'Are times tough? Listen, in Philadelphia they're sucking cocks for food.'

PROSTITUTION

342. ALASKA (Doncaster, Lancaster, Master). Added line limerick. Compare Limericks 188 (Vol. II) and 631 (this volume). Variant: 'But when she got spliced' (1927).

343. *Coitus Saxonius*, a contraceptive measure described in Magnus Hirschfeld's *Sexualkunde*, effected by clamping a thumb and forefinger over the base of the man's penis just as he begins to ejaculate, forcing the semen into the bladder. The hateful elements are of course obvious.

344.   The tail of her shirty
        Was also quite dirty   [1927

355. On Miss Belle da Costa Greene, the elder Morgan's librarian.

363. Polluted proverb: 'If at first you don't succeed – keep sucking!' (1940).

365. On a popular song of the 1920s; ultimately from Swinburne's masochist ballad, 'Dolores'.

367. A reply to the rising prices of Limericks 342, and 376.

370. Typical catch: two outer persons of three walking abreast, ask each other: 'Do you feel like a ball?' (Both answer yes.) 'Then there must be a prick between us.' 'No, a prick is a part of a man!'

373. JAIPUR (Cawnpore, Debwar, Jodhpur, Lahore, Tanjore). Compare Limericks 175, 183 and 395 in Vol. II.

374. Joan Bennett: a movie-star of the period, apparently kinder than most. U.S.O. (United Service Organization): 'A civilian movement for giving cookies to soldiers in need of a screw.'

378.   She took her sarong
          And wrapped up each dong,
       And sent it on an explorative tour.   [1942

385. The last line a parody of Villon's 'Mais où sont les neiges d'antan' (But where are the snows of yore?)

388. Chinatown price-list from Herbert Asbury's *The Barbary Coast* (1933), p. 177: 'Two bittee lookee, flo bittee feelee, six bittee doee!' (a bit being an imaginary coin worth $12\frac{1}{2}$ cents), preceded by 'China girl nice! You come inside, please?' to which is 'invariably added . . . this extraordinary information seldom, if ever, correct: "Your father, he just go out!" ' to which Asbury adds the pre-analytic note: 'Some of the Chinese considered it an honor to possess a woman whom their fathers had also possessed.' (Apocryphal Shanghai brothel-sign: 'Sholt-time piecee – 1 buck Mex. Long-time piecee – 1 buck 'Melican. Ass-hole flee if stay all night.')

390. Said a naked young sailor, named Chuck,
       To his cunt, 'Kid, I'm shit out of luck.

I'm due back at the dock,
   But I've got a stiff cock;
Spread your legs, and I'll throw you a fuck.'

[1951

393. Compare Limerick 563 in Vol. II.

395. This is the first recorded erotic limerick, printed in *Cythera's Hymnal, or Flakes from the Foreskin* ('Oxford', 1870), p. 70, headed 'Nursery Rhymes', and followed by fifty others, to p. 82. *Poor*, in the last line, is to be pronounced dialectally, *pore*.

399. *That Immoral Garland* (1942) noting, 'This is from Ovid', which, though unlikely, points up the direct line of descent of the limerick from the obscene verse epigrams of the Greek Anthology, Martial, and other satirists of the Graeco-Roman period, through Antonio Beccadelli of Palermo (d. 1471, to whose *Hermaphroditus*, or collection of erotic epigrams, the more famous *Manual of Classical Erotology* of Forberg – Latin original, 1824 – is merely a commentary), to the *Sinngedichte* of Lessing (d. 1781) Bk. II: 'The unjust mob falsely imputed love of boys to the righteous Turan. To chastise the lies what else could he do but – sleep with his sister.'

407. During World War II in the United States, new automobiles were purportedly difficult to buy.

410. Compare Limerick 402 in Vol. II. Variant:

   And if you don't mind
   You may try my behind –

[1927

411. A well-known joke (spoonerism) in limerick form. Note telegraphic answer: ten words.

412. – She's a Salvation Army lass now.

[1949

414. SWOBODA (Baroda, Bogota, Dakota, Pajoder, Minnesota, Rhoda). With variants: 'So she jumped from the couch In a

helluva grouch', 'She grew very sore, Rose up from the floor'
(1948A); 'So she wiggled her ass To the edge of his glass, And
crapped in his whiskey and soda' (1942).

416. Variant: 'With her kith and her kin, She lay writhing in sin.'
Compare Limerick 938 in Vol. II.

418.   As if in a trance
        She pulled off her pants   [1950

        In the manner of whores
        She never wore drawers
    And he sucked all his spunk from her orifice.

                                                                    [1943B

420. On the legend of the 'knowledgeful whore', see the lost love-
books of the Greek and Roman matriarch-prostitutes
(hetaira) listed in Iwan Bloch's *Die Prostitution*. One magnificent 'restoration' of a 'lost' love-book of this sort is *Die
Weisheiten der Aspasia* by 'Fritz Thurn' [Fritz Foregger]
privately printed in Vienna, 1923, probably the finest erotic
work since Chorier's *Luisa Sigea* (*c.* 1659).

421. Joke of the impotent old man who married an acrobat: she'd
stand on her head and he'd drop it in.

422. Compare Limerick 270 in Vol. II. Variant:
    While sucking her grandfather's prick,
        Exclaimed, 'I don't funk
        The taste of your spunk
    It's the smell of your arse makes me sick.'   [1882

423. YALE (Gale, Grail, Hale, MacPhail, Marseille, St. Gail,
Thrale). One of the most popular limericks in America over
the last decade. Publicly published in *Peter Pauper's Limerick
Book* (ed. 1942), and in William DuBois' *The Island in the
Square* (1947) p. 186, with the remark: 'Let's swap limericks,
and enjoy ourselves for a change.' Variant: 'On the tits of a
hooker named Gale, Was tattooed the price of her tail'
(1946A). Homosexual variant: 'On the chest of a gob from
Marseille' (1951).

DISEASES

424. A sequel to Limerick 1.

426.   The slimy green cheese
       Hung down to her knees
And congealed at the end of her drawers.   [1941A

427. BANKER (Bangkor, Casablanca, Salamanca). Compare Limericks 1098 and 1116.

428. A variant published, as 'Venereal Ode,' in the 'Tonics and Sedatives' department of the *Journal of the American Medical Association* (31 January 1942), v. 118: no. 5: p. 24, with Jesus expurgated to Croesus (!) in the last stanza; lacking the fifth stanza here, and with the sixth thus:

He aches from his head to his toes,
His sphincters have gone where who knows,
     Paradoxal incontinence
     With all its concomitance
Brings forth unpredictable flows.

440. CHESTER (DePeyster, Esther, Hester, Leicester, Nor'wester, Port Chester, Winchester). See 930 in Vol. II*.

443. Variant conclusions: 'I must have a D-O-S-E' (1934), 'As he banged his jappap on his knee' (1946A). Drake (1949) finds in the couplet an 'elaborately disguised pun on the English meaning of the word "pax" '. (Street preacher: 'Peace on you, brother'. Italian peddler: 'Pees on you too, you sona-vabitch!') *Cleopatra's Scrapbook* (1928) p. iii, varies the following version:

'I have'e God Dam'ee hard'ee.'

There was once a heathen Chinee
Who went out in the Backyard to Pee.
     Said he, 'What is thisee?
     My cockee no pissee,
Hellee, God Damee, chordee.'   [1928A

There was a young man from St. Trap
Who contracted a dose of the clap.
   He said, '*Pax vobiscum*,
   Why don't my piss come?
These nuns are too much for a chap!' [1952

447. The earliest politico-erotic limerick. Compare Limericks 407 and 581 (Vol. II), 220 and 242 (this volume). A bitter anti-Semitic caricature and editorial (ending with the accusation of dirtiness – compare Note 610 in Vol. II) appears in *Vanity Fair* (London, 19 October 1872) 'Statesmen, No. 127'.

448. Crabless in Gaza.

451.   'You've stolen my wealth,
    You've ruined my health' [1943

    'You cost all I had
    And it wasn't half bad,
But now you've quit fucking, you fool!' [1939A

461. Parodying the song 'My Home in Tennessee'. In *Preface to an Unprintable Opus* ['Christopher Columbo'] by 'Pedro Pococampo' (Walter Klinefelter; Portland, Maine, 1942), p. 4, an even shorter fragment is given, Mr. Klinefelter re-collecting privately (1944) a section of the stanzaic portion – not in the limerick metre – from hearing it sung 'about 25 years ago':

    The doctors round the door
    They to each other swore
    They never saw before
    Such a tool as I wore.

465.   His *cojones* were furious
    For pleasures injurious [1941

Cojones furiosos: 'hot nuts'. A limerick version of the opening stanza of a well-known ballad, 'The Spanish Nobilio', of which the tune is similar to that to which limericks are sung.

467. Joke of the Negro mother who names her children SyPHILis
and GoNORRhea, explaining that she found these pretty
names on their birth certificates.

470. Unpleasant schoolboy versions, such as this, of the standard
womb-return fantasy are common. Joke (Pa., *c.* 1925), on
two big Irish icemen who cannot make the widow come, but
the little wizened Jew can, explaining: 'I just stuck my head
in and puked.'

473. Frank Harris, *My Life* (Nice, 1925), v. 2: p. 362.

474. 'Red-lined' and '35–1440' refer to the withholding of U.S.
Army ('G.I.') pay because of venereal disease.

476. Capivi (*copaiba*): a remedy for gonorrhea.

477.   Said the girls, 'Oh my gosh,
        You really must wash'   [1952

        They said, 'You old dub,
        You really must scrub'   [1949

478. Variants: 'And she valued so highly, Each *membrum virile*'
(1939A; compare Limerick 789 in Vol. II), 'She should have
known better Than to refuse a French letter' (1946B).

        Their pricks she oft sucked,
        Was oft buggered and fucked,
     And at last came to grief – for the pox ate her.

                                                                [1870

479. Safe: a condom, called 'French safes' in *Jim Jam Jems* (N.
Dakota, September 1916), p. 23. Joke: 'These condoms are
guaranteed. – What happens if they break? – The guarantee
runs out.'

LOSSES

485. BATES (Gates, States, Yates). Variants: 'A Russian sword-
dancer' (1951), 'A young pirate named Bates, Was fencing
one day with his mates' (1950). Joke, on a gentleman named
Bates introducing his family to Abraham Lincoln: 'My wife,
Mrs. Bates; my daughter, Miss Bates; and my son, Master
Bates.' Lincoln: 'Why brag about it?'

490. Austin: a diminutive automobile of the 1930s.

> His balls hung so low
> That they swung to and fro,
> And got caught on a rock and he lost 'em.   [1950

492. Compare the lines by Francis Jeffrey, editor of the *Edinburgh
Review* (1803–29) and author of the devastating criticism of
Wordsworth's *The Excursion* (1814) beginning 'This will
never do': 'On Peter Robinson – Here lies the preacher,
judge and poet, Peter, Who broke the laws of God, and man,
and metre.'

494. 'I don't like to see – it's a fact that I utter That nasty word
[CUNT] written up on a shutter; And I don't like to see a
man, drunk as an Earl, Getting into a lamp-post thinking it's
a girl.' –

The Pearl, no. 17 (November 1880), the 13th of 15 verses
titled 'Things I don't like to see'. (The present limerick had
appeared in number 1 of *The Pearl*.) Compare the exactly
similar quatrains of Pierre Louÿs' posthumous *Pybrac* (1928),
each of the 256 examples beginning, 'Je n'aime pas à voir . . .'

> There was a young man from Wamsutter
> Who attempted to shit on a shutter.
> > There were roars of dismay
> > When the shutter gave way,
> And he finished his shit in the gutter.   [1952

495. Joke, involving 'holes in the penis of a war veteran, who is
recommended to see a piccolo teacher, who will teach him to

"finger that stump" so he won't urinate on strangers. Under the pretence of mere callousness, a second castration ("veteran's re-education" by the piccolo teacher) is clearly contemplated.' – G. Legman, 'Rationale of the Dirty Joke', *Neurotica*, no. 9 (1951), p. 59.

A Wagnerian tenor named Knut
Sailed a brig from Bayreuth to Beirut.
   [*Couplet from Limerick* 485]
Now he sings in duets with a flute.   [1944

499. The fantasy of the chastity-belt (infibulation: female castration) here combined with castration of the male. That the chastity-belt is a fantasy, and has no historical existence, will not be argued here.

500. [Aleister Crowley], *White Stains: The Literary Remains of George Archibald Bishop, a Neuropath of the Second Empire* (1898), p. 10: 'One flash alone illumines the darkness of his boyhood; in 1853, after being prepared for confirmation, he cried out in full assembly, instead of kneeling to receive the blessing of the officiating bishop, "I renounce for ever this idolatrous church"; and was quietly removed.'

505. CREEK (Barking Creek, East Creek, Peek, West Creek, Wokingham Creek). Variant in the couplet: WOKING (Hoboken).

508. Limerick version of the poem 'Screwy Dick with the Spiral Prick'. *Index Limericus* notes: 'The boar pig takes his time very leisurely, his penis being of a corkscrew shape.' – William Acton, *The Functions and Disorders of the Reproductive Organs* (1858), p. 30.

513. 'Beaver!' (also 'Zitz!'): a street cry when a beard is seen. Variant:

Filled up the bath tub to receive her;
   She took off her clothes
   From her head to her toes,
And a voice at the keyhole yelled, 'Beaver!'   [1927

514. Parodying the limerick-metre poem 'The Time I've Lost in Wooing' by Thomas Moore (*c.* 1810), with an obvious pun in 'on the whole'. Variant: 'By wearing my drawers While climbing on whores.'

515. Compare the long-penis castration story of the man who takes too strong an aphrodisiac, whereupon his penis grows so long that it follows a girl across the street and up the stairs '– and here comes the STREETCAR!' Variant:

> Who claimed he could smell cunt a block away.
>   He picked up a quiff
>   Who gave him the syph,
> And it rotted the tip of his cock away.   [1945A

516. Other two-line attempts: 711* (this volume), 867 (Vol. II).

517. A joke, 'The Patience of Job', in *The Pearl*, no. 5 (November 1879), about a farmer reprimanded for swearing by his wife, with a reminder of the patience of Job. 'Blast that damned Job ... he never had his balls caught in a rabbit trap!' A. Irving Hallowell, 'Aggression in Saulteaux Society', in *Psychiatry* (1940), v. 3: p. 395–407: 'Some years ago ... several Berens River Indians who were out hunting came upon the traps of an Indian of the Sandy Lake Band ... One of the hunters, egged on by his companions, defecated on one of the traps. Then he sprung the trap so that a piece of feces was left sticking out. Such an act was an insult to the owner of the trap and a deterrent to any animal that might approach it.' Compare Limerick 537.

> There was a young fellow named Bell
> Whose tale is heart-breaking to tell.
>   He once took a crap
>   In the woods, and a trap
> Underneath – oh, it's tragic as hell!   [1941

522. Printed on a U.S. comic post card (Boston, Mass.: Tichnor Bros., no. 651, *ante* 1948).

524. 'YES! We Have No Bananas' (1923), a phenomenally successful castratory 'nonsense' song. Compare Limericks 630, 700.

525. Attributed to the Hollywood biographer, Gene Fowler (a version without the second and third choruses), as is a remarkable castration novelette, *The Demi-Wang* by 'Peter Long' (New York: Privately Printed, 1931). This work is casually discussed in Herbert Kerkow's *The Fateful Star Murder* (1931), pp. 197–8. It contains probably the largest number of nonce-synonyms for the penis and sexual intercourse to be found in any fictional piece in English. (Compare the strikingly similar erotic verbalization in the castration poem, *The Loves of Hero and Leander*, 1651, by J[ames] S[mith].) Both 'Anne Cooper Hewitt' – first published as 'The Sterilized Heiress' in *Unexpurgated* (1943), p. 45, and based on a newspaper sensation of the 1930s – and *The Demi-Wang* contain satirical references to the actress Mary Pickford, whose book *The Demi-Widow* is parodied in the title.

533.   Who suffered from inguinal hernia.
       When offered a truss
       He said with a cuss,
'Just you mind the things that concern you.'   [1870

The text-form printed in Samuel Hopkins Adams' *A. Woollcott: his life and his world* (1945), p. 122, as Heywood Broun's 'unprinted surgical limerick' (d. 1939).

534. *That Immoral Garland* (1942), noting it as 'another instance of the enduring quality of that silly legend' as to the obliquity of the Oriental vagina. Compare Limericks 198, 765, 902, 925 in Vol. II.

536. King Jonathan Edward the third
     Was caught pederasting a bird.
         He'd rammed the thing through
         With his long, slender screw,
     And had pushed out a seven-inch turd.   [1952

538. Emperor Haile Selassie of Ethiopia, called 'The Lion of Judah', driven from his throne by Mussolini in 1936.

539. Noted in *Neurotica*, no. 9 (1951), p. 53, as a minced version of the vagina-dentata threat.
  Who was stuck for a week by the belly
    To a Jew who used glue,
      When he wanted to screw   [1944A

546. Compare Limerick 374 in Vol. II. The psychoanalytic literature is rich in references to the sun as father-figure. See, in particular, 'The Blazing Sun: A psychoanalytic Approach to Van Gogh' by Jacques Schnier, in *American Imago* (July 1950), reprinted in *Neurotica*, no. 8 (1951).

548. See Note 414 in Vol. II.

553.   She took down her britches,
      Said, 'Ouch, but it itches'.   [1948

555. Of the iambic-idiotic school. Note the suicidal-sadistic self-directed violence obviously intended for the bride.

557. Compare Limerick 445.

559. A version printed in an Army joke-book, *Keep 'Em Laughing* (N.Y., 1942) by William Allan Brooks, captioned, 'Sic Transit Gloria Mundi'.

565. On the gardener, see *Genesis* 3:8.

566. The original, and less sadistic version of Limerick 316. Horace Fletcher: an American businessman and nutrition crank who taught the thorough mastication – 'fletcherizing' – of every mouthful of food.

570. Compare Limerick 542. Variant: 'My God!' he exclaimed, 'I perceive I am maimed.'   [1943A

571.   In attempting to bugger
      A boy on a lugger   [1932

573. Compare Limerick 325, and Notes 272, 291 in Vol. II.

578. Castration fantasy, parodying Gelett Burgess' famous 'On Digital Extremities' (1901), itself a symbolization of the same fears.

579. Rhymeless (anti-authoritarian: compare Whitman). On the fear of the Atom Bomb, the castratory nature of which is popularly perceived only as fear of 'sterilization' after-effects. Compare the classic womb-return fantasy, with the incestuous element boldly prominent, in 'The Wish' by the Earl of Rochester (d. 1680):

> Oh, that I now cou'd by some Chymick Art
> To Sperm convert my Vitals and my Heart,
> That in one thrust I might my Soul translate,
> And in the Womb my self regenerate:
> There steep'd in Lust, nine Months I wou'd remain,
> Then boldly fuck my Passage out again.

583. Joke, about married men on a hunting trip, none of whom could get to sleep until the guide gave each of them a hairbrush to hold.

SEX SUBSTITUTES

587. Variant: 'And part of a tit out in Dallas' (1946B). Protracted ballad of the dynamiting of a pregnant woman's vagina by two obstetricians, 'The Ballad of Chambers Street', by Dr. Fritz Irving, with the climactic stanza: 'Proud Aetna in her salad days, on that Sicilian shore, Did not erupt much more abrupt than did that Hebrew whore. With mangled child she much defiled the waters of the bay; His balls fell short of Cambridge port; his cod struck there to stay.'

591. Compare Limericks 225, 241.

599. The first limerick printed in *The Pearl*, no. 1 (July 1879),
captioned 'Nursery Rhymes'. Often printed and collected
since.

604. See Note 546.

611.   She said, 'A bologna
       Is the real corona,
Because it never gets soft.'   [1927

619.   There once was a dissolute monk
Who fell asleep on a trunk.
      He dreamt that Venus
      Was pulling his penis,
And woke up all covered with gunk.   [1941

622. Is not just a super-sensorium.   [1952

625.   He lined it with hair
      And fucked it with care   [1941

       Into which he would stick
       His episcopal prick   [1945

627. Query: 'encompass'?

629.   To jizz-jazzm-spasm
      She had her orgasm
At least twice as quickly – but natch!   [1952

There was a young woman named Margo
Who came when they played Handel's Largo.
      But when they played Liszt
      She farted and pissed
Just to show what she thought of such cargo.   [1952

There is a young lady named Hatch
Who constantly scratches her snatch.
      'Tis not for sensation
      Of sweet masturbation,
But because of some crabs she can't catch.   [1943A

633.   His fly-buttons busted
         And he ran home disgusted   [1952

634. 'All there': the threatened insanity of masturbation, plus the
     equally traditional threat of castration.

637. Limerick version (made abysmally worse in *Unexpurgated*,
     1943A) of a joke far more succinct: Homosexual (*to whore*):
     'Prostitute!' Whore (*to homosexual*): 'Substitute!'

     A fancy young pansy, Paul Potts,
     Met a whore in a store down in Watts.
         Sneered the queer, 'Shoo, you floosie!'
         Roared the whore, 'Don't be choosy!
     After all, my dear Paul, you're ersatz!'   1943A

640. Compare Limerick 600.

641.   She neighed like a filly
         'Cause it tickled her silly,
         And kept her ass warm in cold weather.   [1951

645. Compare Note 629.

650. Morse (1948) p. 138, notes: 'There is a case recorded of a
     man who masturbated in his sleep. He had a wire cage made
     in which he locked himself at night by strapping it around his
     middle, and throwing the key onto the floor. (Max Hühner,
     Sexual Debility in Man, pp. 103–4.) This prevented him from
     giving it that last lick.'

651.   When he pulls out his needle
         They yell, 'Hi, diddle deedle,
         This is no fag, but a fay.'   [1942

657.   She used a dill pickle,
         Explaining, 'The tickle
         Is swell till the warts wear away.'   [1941

660. To fuck herself silly
        With the stem of a lily,
      And sit on a sunflower to piss.   [1928A

664. He did it by hand
        With a synthetic gland
      Which he hid in the folds of his tunic.   [1943A

666. NORWAY (Bombay, Calais, Cambrai, Cape May, Great Bay,
      Hudson's Bay).
        As his penis arose
        The temperature froze
      And he shot a vanilla frappé.   [1952

668. Compare Limericks 354 (Vol. II) and 587, 661 (this volume).

669. From the Dawn Club, San Francisco, 1946. Compare
     Limerick 609.

670. By P[hilip] H[eseltine], in *The Week-End Book* (London:
     Nonesuch Press, ed. 1927), p. 157, captioned 'The Jung Idea'.
     In the 1928 edition 'old-fashioned' becomes 'long-standing'.
     Douglas (1928), p. 80, spells out the pun on 'phalluses', with
     a delicious burlesque Freudian letter. *Index Limericus* notes
     the source of the rhymes here in Gilbert and Sullivan's
     Gondoliers (1889):

        I'm aware you object
          To pavilions and palaces,
        But you'll find I respect
          Your Republican fallacies.   (Act I, *ad fin.*)

671. One of the most popular limericks. Compare the surprise
     ending of Limerick 98 in Vol. II. Usually ends, 'Your gher-
     kin's for ferkin', not jerkin'.' Also: 'You're shirking your
     furking – get working, John Perkins!' (1939A). The rhymes
     are perhaps inevitable ('Of course, five cents in those days …
     bought a firkin of gherkins or a ramekin of fescue or a pipkin
     of halvah' – S. J. Perelman, 'So little time marches on,' in his
     Keep It Crisp, 1946, p. 49), but the ultimate source may well

be the limerick-metre 'Song to Ceres' by Leigh Hunt (d. 1859),
published in Emerson's *Parnassus* (1875):

> Laugh out in the loose green jerkin
> That's fit for a goddess to work in,
>   With shoulders brown
>   And the wheaten crown
> About thy temples perking . . .

Index Limericus marvellously notes Dexter Perkins' history
of the Monroe Doctrine, called *Hands Off* (Boston, 1941).

678. RACINE (McLean). This is the limerick most frequently
encountered in this research. The principal variant endings
are given in the text as 679. First publicly printed in 'The
Human Machine' by John Del Torto, in *Neurotica*, no. 8
(1951), p. 23, delicately modified to a 'screwing machine',
and with the clank-mechanical ending: 'And could wank
itself off in between.' Del Torto also gives, as analogue, a
passage from Thomas Nash, his *Dildo* (MS. 1601), first
printed in John S. Farmer's *Merry, Facetious, and Witty
Songs and Ballads* (1895) [v. 1:], p. 22:

'He bendeth not, nor fouldeth any deale, but standes as stiffe
as he were made of steele; (And playes at peacock twixt my
leggs right blithe And doeth my tickling swage with manie a
sighe;) And when I will, he doth refresh me well, and never
makes my tender belly swell.' Poore Priapus, thy kingdom
needes must fall . . .

The theme of the sex machine has a long history and a com-
plex psychological background which cannot be handled
here. But see Victor Tausk's 'On the Origin of the "Influenc-
ing Machine" in Schizophrenia' (1919) translated in *Psychoanalytic Quarterly* (1933) and abridged in *Neurotica*, no. 8
(1951) with additional notes of relevance to science fiction.
Examples of the sex machine fantasy will be found in De
Nerciat's *Les Aphrodites* (1793), in 'The New Patent Fucking
Machine', a ballad at the end of v. 2 of *The Pearl*, no. 12
(June 1880), in Eddy Smith's *Zehn Radierungen* (Berlin,
1921) – drawings of forms for both male and female, reprinted in the 'Ergänzender Bilderteil' to Hirschfeld and

Linsert's *Liebesmittel* (Berlin, 1930) – in *Memoirs of a Russian Princess* 'by Katoumbah Pasha' (London–Paris, 1890), Pt. 6, the machine being named Belphegor [!]; in two pictorial 'novelties' circulated in the U.S. about 1930 and 1940: 'The Delighter' (on a Ford chassis), and the 'Rape-all' (with cunt-lapper and titsucker 'Attachments' on the style of the present limerick); in a modern ballad, 'The Great Wheel' (to the hymn-tune: 'Oh Master, Let Me Walk With Thee'), beginning: 'A sailor told me ere he died, I don't know whether the bastard lied, His wife had had a cunt so wide, She never could ever be satisfied' (Yale, 1939); and in Limericks 743 (Vol. II) and 101, 680, and limerick-sequence 685 here. Among the endless other curiosa of the subject may be mentioned the novel *The Magnificent MacInnes* (1949) by Shepherd Mead, pocket reprinted (*c.* 1951) as *The Sex Machine*. (And see Drake's colophon in the bibliography here.)

Il y avait un jeune homme de Boyer
Qui fabrique une machine à futoyer.
   Concave ou convexe,
   Pour plaire aux deux sexes,
Et extrêmement simple à nettoyer   [1941

Homo ingenius Racina
Coitus invenit machina.
   Adapta convexus
   Utrosque pro sexus
Dispendit cum omne vagina.   [1941

682. 'her hot hole': compare the opening line of John Marston's *The Insatiate Countesse* (1613): 'What should we doe in this Countesses darke hole?'

696.   It arose to a stand
       And insisted his hand
    Should caress it and play pocket-pool.   [1942

703.   When asked if he screwed
       He replied that he would,
    But he greatly preferred masturbation.   [1943

704. Oliver St. John Gogarty, *As I Was Going Down Sackville Street* (N.Y., 1937) chap. vi, p. 113: 'I am deep in the folklore of the churn . . . the awful tragedy of it is that no one realizes what is being lost. The sea chanties were nearly all gone until a few late-comers collected half-a-dozen Bowdlerised stanzas or so. But the churn! Only one song of buttermaking remains . . . Father Claude overheard it in Tipperary, when a buxom maid was churning, as she thought, all alone. She had buttocks like a pair of beautiful melons. Her sleeves were rolled up. She had churned from early morning. Her neck was pink with exercise. Her bosom laboured, but she could not desist, for the milk was at the turn. Up and down, desperately she drove the long handle: up and down, up and down and up and up for a greater drive. The resistance grew against the plunger. Her hips and bosom seemed to increase in size while her waist grew thin. In front of her ears the sweat broke into drops of dew. She prayed in the crisis to the old forgotten gods of the homestead! Twenty strokes for ten! Gasping, she sang:

> "Come, butter!
> Come, butter!
> Come, butter,
> Come!
> Every lump
> As big as
> My bum!" '

708.   And fixed her thoughts on the sublime.   [1952

710. Variants: La Platte, Spratt, Tatt; 'the village idiot sat'. Compare Limerick 1672.

There was a young fellow named Pratt
Who was terribly sassy and fat   [1944A

There once was a priest, Father Pat,
Who would roar out the *Magnificat*   [1943B

711. Unfinishable variant (or two-line limerick, compare 516) proposed at the American Limerick Society, *c.* 1944:

> There was a young girl from Vancouver
> Who was raped by President Hoover.

712. He woke screaming defiance
Of religion and science [1952

714. Morse (1948), p. 140, noting this as a short-lived patriotic number of World War II on the various U.S. Women's Auxiliary Corps, adds 'the story about the men who were comparing notes. One asked, "Which would you rather have: A Wac in a shack, A Spar in a car, or a Wave in a cave?" The other replied, "A sheep in a jeep".' Add (*c.* 1944) the soldier who was busted out of the service for putting Wacs on the floor, and the sailor who was sucked under the board-walk by a big Wave.

716. As she felt his cock swell
She exclaimed, 'What the hell!'
So he went to the doctor's to dock it. [1942

ADDENDA

741. My occupation after dark
Is goosing statues in the park
If Sherman's horse can take it
Why can't you?

('Humoresque', 1944A)

744. Clean original illustrated in A. B. Frost's *Stuff and Nonsense* (1888), p. 89. Compare Burton's note on the man-cannon or *Adami-top*, his rectum loaded with peppercorns and fired by a pinch of snuff applied to the nose, in the *Arabian Nights*, v. 10: pp. 235–6. (Burton Club ed., v. 10: pp. 203–4.)

747. 1930s wit in this contretemps: 'Pardon my Southern accent.' (From a Gracie Allen erotic cartoon booklet.)

748. The identity of money and feces par excellence.

760. Vying with Limerick 87.

761. 'derrière': advertising cant for arse.

762. The Little Red Hen and rooster are protagonists of various non-limerick folk verses.

766. 'This big chimpanzee
    Is a comfort to me –'   [1952

    'This ape has a lingam
    That's something to swing on –'   [1952

767. Reversing the direction of entry in the usual long-penis and bride jokes: 'Be careful dear; you know my weak heart. – I'll go easy passing the heart.' Also: 'Deep enough? – No, deeper – Deep enough now? – No, deeper! – *Now* is it deep enough? – Ugg ugg.' With this 'sadistic concept of coitus' compare Limerick 87 (*en brochette* in Tibet).

768. On the series of advertisements showing two women posed with, and handling each other, captioned 'Which twin has the Toni?' (a brand of hair-wave), which gave the go-ahead to open Lesbianism in American advertising since World War II. A novelty card, so captioned, shows twin girls in a bathtub with an Italian plumber.

775. F. L. Wells, in *American Imago* (March 1951) v. 8: p. 93, quotes a similar 'Frau Wirtin' verse (the German counterpart of the English-language limerick – see Hayn-Gotendorf-Englisch, *Bibliotheca Germanorum Erotica et Curiosa*, 1929, v. 9: pp. 632–3, 'Das Wirtshaus an der Lahn'):

    Frau Wirtin hatte 'nen Student
    Der war in furzen ein Talent.
    Er furzt' 'Die letzte Rose,'
    Doch als der Sang an Aegir kam
    Da schiss er in die Hose.

776. Many examples of 'The Anal Character' hardly less absurd are cited by Karl Abraham, *Selected Papers* (1927), pp. 383–6. And compare Note 132.

777. 'Folklore aside ... rabbis do not customarily perform circumcisions, this being done by a minor functionary called a *mohel*, self-appointed to the work.' – G. Legman, in *Neurotica* (1951), no. 9, p. 59.

780. Screwy Dick (Limerick 508) revised.

781. The Hermit of the Mohave (Limerick 349 in Vol. II) revised for an oral-neurotic generation. See Note 261 in Vol. II.

783. The first literary product of the Korean War.

INDEX

Asterisks refer to variants in the Notes

Stimulating Reading from Panther Books

Fascinating Non-fiction Reading in Panther Books

All-action Fiction from Panther

THE IPCRESS FILE	Len Deighton	50p	☐
AN EXPENSIVE PLACE TO DIE	Len Deighton	50p	☐
DECLARATIONS OF WAR	Len Deighton	35p	☐
A GAME FOR HEROES	James Graham*	40p	☐
THE WRATH OF GOD	James Graham*	40p	☐
THE KHUFRA RUN	James Graham*	40p	☐
THE SCARLATTI INHERITANCE			
	Robert Ludlum	60p	☐
THE OSTERMAN WEEKEND	Robert Ludlum	50p	☐
THE MATLOCK PAPER	Robert Ludlam	60p	☐
THE BERIA PAPERS	Alan Williams†	50p	☐
THE TALE OF THE LAZY DOG	Alan Williams†	50p	☐
THE PURITY LEAGUE	Alan Williams†	50p	☐
SNAKE WATER	Alan Williams†	50p	☐
LONG RUN SOUTH	Alan Williams†	50p	☐
BARBOUZE	Alan Williams†	50p	☐
FIGURES IN A LANDSCAPE	Barry England	50p	☐
THE TOUR	David Ely	40p	☐
THEIR MAN IN THE WHITE HOUSE	Tom Ardies	35p	☐
COLD WAR IN A COUNTRY GARDEN			
	Lindsay Gutteridge	30p	☐
KILLER PINE	Lindsay Gutteridge	50p	☐
LORD TYGER	Philip José Farmer	50p	☐

*The author who 'makes Alistair Maclean look like a beginner' (*Sunday Express*)

†'The natural successor to Ian Fleming' (*Books & Bookmen*)

Real-life Adventure and Violence in Panther Books